Growing Up in an Immigrant Household and Community

Essays by Descendants of Immigrants

Edited by Vicky Giouroukakis

Cover image © Shutterstock.com

www.innovativeinkpublishing.com
Send all inquiries to:
4050 Westmark Drive
Dubuque, IA 52004-1840

Copyright © Vasiliki (Vicky) Giouroukakis

ISBN: 9-798-7657-6383-4

All rights reserved. No part of this publication may be reproduced, stored in a retrieval system, or transmitted, in any form or by any means, electronic, mechanical, photocopying, recording, or otherwise, without the prior written permission of the copyright owner.

Published in the United States of America

To my parents, Polychronis and Constantina, and my grandmother, Vasiliki, who advised and taught me by example that with hard work, determination, and perseverance, I can achieve my goals.

To my fiercest supporter and cheerleader, my husband John Giouroukakis, whose gentle and wise guidance always steers me in the right direction. The son of Greek immigrants Emanuel and Anna, he has also both enjoyed the pleasures and endured the hardships that the immigrant experience entails.

To all the children and grandchildren of immigrants all over the world, including my own children—Emanuel, Anna, Paul. Never forget who your ancestors are and where they came from, all the sacrifices they made, and the gifts they have given you so that you and your descendants can have a better life than they did.

Contents

Editor's Essay xiii

    Straddling Two Worlds: Defining My Greek-American Identity
    Vicky Giouroukakis xxv

Section 1: Challenges and Hardships 1

On Being Armenian 3
    [Armenian]
    Aida Zilelian

It Didn't Have to Be This Way: The Consequences of Strict Immigrant Parents 7
    [Colombian]
    Patricia Lozano Miller

Il Dolce (The Sweet) 11
    [Italian]
    Milena Perna Scalzo

Save, Save, Save 14
    [Italian]
    Alfredo Vinci

Alphabet   17
   [Greek]
   Terry Stratoudakis

Garlic   21
   [Iranian]
   Nazli Diba

Distant Memories   24
   [Uzbek] [Student Essay]
   Polina Oleynikova

Section 2: Fond Childhood Memories of the Immigrant Community   27

Authentic Trilingual NYC Upbringing and Immersion into Sicilian Roots   29
   [Italian; Mexican]
   Silvia Rosselli Davi

Treasure Island, the Bronx   33
   [Mixed-European]
   Jean Ende

My Birthday   38
   [Greek]
   Vicky Giouroukakis

Bajan Memories: Always in My Heart   42
   [Bajan: Barbadian]
   Joy Scantlebury

Summers in Greece   48
   [Greek]
   Nadia Giannopoulos

Section 3: The Immigrant Household and Food 51

Mamma Dina: Food as Love 53
[Greek]
Vicky Giouroukakis

The Culinary Cardinal 58
[Italian]
Maria C. Palmer

Rice Ball Stick Together 63
[Taiwanese]
Cindy (Ai-Ling) Li

First-Generation Persian-Jewish-American Family Thanksgivings and Blessings 67
[Persian-Jewish]
Rebecca Yousefzadeh Sassouni

Section 4: Life Lessons Learned from Immigrant Parents 69

A Letter of Gratitude 71
[Irish]
Maggie Blair

The Values Instilled in Me by My Parents 75
[Ghanaian]
Gloria Serwa Gyimah

My Parents' Ultimate Sacrifice 79
[Greek]
Fiffy Eliades

Practicality 83
[Irish]
Noreen Williams

Ode to Glendita 87
    [Honduran]
    Ashley Tavormina

Better than a Thousand Sons 90
    [Indian; Pakistani]
    Mubina Schroeder

Guidance from a Guyanese Mother 94
    [Guyanese]
    Nadia Khan-Roopnarine

Mother and Children Discuss Immigrant Experiences 99
    [Jamaican]
    Sherone Smith-Sánchez and Her Children

Section 5: Life Lessons Learned from Immigrant Grandparents 105

Opposites Attract 107
    [Irish; Croatian]
    Joanne O'Brien

My Immigrant Grandparents 111
    [Mixed-European]
    Rickey Moroney

Greek Women in the Family 114
    [Greek]
    Peggy Pyrovolakis

***Yiayia* 118**
    [Greek]
    Matina Stergiopoulos

The Immigrant Hustle 122
     [Italian]
     Tim Roda

My Grandfather, the Legend 126
     [Greek] [Student Essay]
     Emanuel Giouroukakis

Growing Up with a Pappou 129
     [Greek] [Student Essay]
     Paul Giouroukakis

How did our immigrant parents do it?
Every holiday was filled with so much joy, food, and gifts.
Our childhoods were defined by their sacrifice and their commitment to family.
We didn't have much, but we had everything.

Adapted from: @DOAImmigrant

A Few Words by Evy Poumpouras

Every immigrant has a story and it's so important to share them. It's how we grow empathy, build bridges, and heal the world. I am so proud of Vicky for bringing these powerful stories to life.

Evy Poumpouras, former Secret Service agent and bestselling author of *Becoming Bulletproof: Protect Yourself, Read People, Influence Situations, and Live Fearlessly.*

Acknowledgments

I would like to acknowledge my husband John, for being my biggest supporter, for offering valuable advice on all aspects of the book from start to finish, for providing meaningful feedback on multiple drafts of my essays when I asked for it (sometimes impatiently and in inopportune times), for allowing me to be consumed by this book project for months, and for patiently and graciously putting up with me throughout the process.

A woman cannot be as good as she could be without the support of another woman. For me, this is Matina Stergiopoulos, who has encouraged me throughout this journey by pushing me along, praising my efforts, generously answering my queries, and commenting on my work—thank you so much!

When I think about model mentors, Dr. Joanne O'Brien comes to mind first. As a successful daughter of immigrants (she also wrote an endearing essay for this book), she inspires me every day with her kind leadership and friendship. Her unwavering belief in my abilities and potential encourages and empowers me to be the best in my professional career. Thank you for your guidance and for contributing to this book!

I would be remiss if I didn't pay tribute to another individual, the epitome of a successful daughter of immigrant parents, Evy Poumpouras, a celebrity living the American Dream! Her fame speaks volumes about her accomplishments. She is an inspiration to us all with her motivational work, her fearless living, her courage and perseverance, and, above all, her kindness and humanity. She accepted to write an endorsement in support of this book, despite her demanding schedule and many commitments, and I am grateful!

Thank you also to those who read and commented on my work—Jeff Ciccone and Aida Zilelian. Special thanks to George Menexas and Paul Menexas for their precise attention to detail and invaluable feedback, and to Becky Tountas and Olga Tsiolis for the meticulous and quick turnaround editing that helped make my writing stronger—I really appreciate it!

I would like to also acknowledge the contributing authors, without whom there would be no book, for coming on this journey with me. Thank you for taking a chance and accepting my invitation to write your stories and to share your stories (and a part of yourselves) with the world!

Thank you to Innovative Ink and Kendall Hunt—namely, Angela Lampe, Lynne Rogers, and Faith Doyle—for believing in this project and seeing it through to completion.

About the Editor and Author

Vicky Giouroukakis (née Vasiliki Menexas), PhD, was born to Greek immigrant parents, Constantina and Polychronis Menexas, and also raised by her strong, tenacious, maternal grandmother, her namesake, who taught her to be tough and resilient. Vicky is bilingual and bicultural. She has strong ties to her Greek heritage and has spent her life promoting a greater understanding of Greek culture and the immigrant experience.

Vicky is a full professor in the School of Education and Human Services at Molloy University, Rockville Centre, New York, where she teaches undergraduate and graduate courses in literacy methods of teaching. She recently accepted the position of director of graduate and postgraduate programs where she hopes to make a positive impact on the institution and contribute to its success.

Prior to her tenure at Molloy, Vicky taught English at a public high school in Queens, New York, and English as a Second Language (ESL) to adolescents and adults. She graduated from NYU with undergraduate degrees in English and American literature and psychology; from Teacher's College, Columbia University with a master's degree in English education; and from the University of Pennsylvania with a PhD in reading, writing/literacy and a master's degree in Teaching English to Speakers of Other Languages (TESOL).

Over the past 17 years, Vicky has published over 60 journal articles and chapters, and has also coauthored four books. She is also the advisor of Molloy's Greek Club. Vicky received the NYSEC Educator of Excellence Award in 2010, the Research Achievement Award from Molloy in 2015, and the President's Medal of Distinguished Service in 2020.

Vicky's volunteer work includes her roles as president of the Archangel Michael Church Greek Language Institute and chairperson of the cooking club that she started in honor of her mom to raise funds for the poor. As an alumna of the University of Pennsylvania, she gives back by volunteering for the Penn Alumni Interview Program. She is also the copresident of the Tower Foundation of Manhasset Inc., a charity that raises funds for Manhasset public schools.

Vicky was born and raised in Astoria, New York, where she spent most of her life, with the exception of her 5-year stint in Athens, Greece when she was a preteen. She now lives in the suburb of Manhasset, New York, with her husband John, a corporate attorney, and their three children—Emanuel (aged 16 years), Anna (aged 15 years), and Paul (aged 12 years)—and cavapoo Ellie (aged 3 years).

Introduction

How the Idea for This Book Was Conceptualized

Perhaps my mother's passing and my impending 50th birthday were the impetus for my rumination and reflection on my Greek immigrant parents and what it was like growing up in an immigrant household. My parents were both born and raised in Greece and then came to the United States in the late 1960s for the promise of the American Dream. Like other immigrants, they struggled to make money, be successful, and create a better life for their three children. They decided to move back to Greece, the homeland they had missed, but regretted their decision and moved back to the United States five years later. They worked hard and made sacrifices, and their three children graduated college, one of whom also received a doctorate. My parents always felt blessed to be embraced by their new country, which gave them so many opportunities to improve their lives. The immigrant struggle has been well documented, and if one does an Internet search on this topic, they will find hundreds of results. Yet there are few books on the experiences of growing up with immigrant parents and grandparents.

Growing up as a first-generation American has its privileges, obviously. We are born in the land of economic opportunity and freedom. I have fond memories growing up in an immigrant community in Astoria, New York: Italian, Greek, and Irish shop owners who knew me by my first name; friendly, caring neighbors who were more like family; playing carefree on the street with other kids on the block; my house always smelling of homecooked Greek meals; big, festive parties that involved incessant dancing and plate breaking; focusing on getting a good education as a means to achieve success in America; using the Greek language as a secret code so that no one else around could understand; going to church and observing religious sacraments; following Greek rituals and traditions that made us feel different from our American friends but at the same time special; and spending summers in grandma's mountain village.

Yet growing up in two or more cultures also comes with a price. Culture defines a person's identity and is shaped by the values, beliefs, and attitudes prevalent at home and in the community. Culture includes food, dress, religion, language, marriage, music, art, customs, beliefs, values, traditions, rituals, routines, and lifestyle—everything we are and do. Whereas immigrant parents know what their cultural background is and understand that America is their adopted country—and have a strong sense of purpose, why they came here and what they need to accomplish, with some being assimilated to American life more easily than others—children of immigrants typically feel suspended between two worlds, the world of their parents and the country in which they are born, both eventually becoming part of their identity.

Most children of immigrants question who they are, where they belong, and who they want to become. How assimilated to American culture are they and what aspects of their parents' cultures do they adopt? Do they learn to speak their parents' language(s) or not (if that is even a choice)? Do they use their parents' language(s), and if so, to what extent and for what purpose? Do they teach the language(s) to their own children one day? What cultural values, rituals, traditions, mores, and ways of life do they adopt and pass on to their children? Do they continue to be faithful to the religion(s) of their parents as they get older or follow their own set of beliefs?

By growing up in an immigrant household, children of immigrants must go through their own challenges and struggles to figure out where they fit in and who they are. Giannis Antetokounmpo says it best in a Nike commercial: "Growing up as the son of immigrants was like straddling two worlds." In Nigeria, he was considered Greek; in Greece, he was Nigerian. Imagine the impact that other people's perceptions of your cultural identity have on you growing up, how you might feel different or be led to feel different, even though you might think you are the same.

For the past few years, I have been watching the comedian Sebastian Maniscalco do his standup comedy about his immigrant father. I have read his memoir and seen him do interviews on talk shows. Besides being entertained, I have also been intrigued by his life, which bears a lot of resemblance to my own upbringing. In a recent interview, Maniscalco talked about his childhood—how his life at home was different from the world in school and how the disconnect made him feel different from his peers. Watching his shows and interviews, and reading about his life have also made me nostalgic for the good ole days and reflective of the challenges of growing up in an immigrant household. Just as Maniscalco was able to pay tribute to his dad through his comedy, so too I always wanted to pay tribute to my parents.

My parents were not professionals, or famous, or made a difference in the world in ways that would get them written up in the local newspaper. I would read about these professionals or famous people (e.g., bankers, attorneys, doctors, researchers, and activists) in *The Herald* and *Neon Magazine*, two Greek-American publications that reported the news and also covered accomplished individuals of Greek heritage. I knew that my parents' picture would never appear in the newspaper, even though, in my eyes, they were accomplishing something special every day of their lives. My friends' parents were also in the same situation—hardworking folks who were making sacrifices so that their children could have a better life than they did. I began to write about my parents (the unsung heroes) and my childhood, and as I wrote about my experiences, I thought to myself, *Wouldn't it be wonderful if other people shared their own stories so that the world can read about our common (but also different) experiences?*

To shed light on the immigrant experience and how it affects the children who are born in the United States, I decided to create an anthology, a collection of essays. I wanted the essays to be written by American-born children or grandchildren of immigrants from all walks of life and different cultural backgrounds who had an interest in sharing their stories. I put out a call for contributions on social media and on my own personal pages and solicited some help from friends to spread the word. I asked for short pieces (about 1,200 words), as I know from experience that many people prefer and much enjoy reading shorter works.

As a former high school English teacher and current teacher educator, I am partial to the flash personal essay and flash memoir, so I solicited stories in these two formats. A flash essay (Nichols, 2015) is very short compared with the classics and is prose that is driven by ideas. It resembles a first-person opinion piece. Flash memoir (Bousquin, 2015), on the other hand, employs the narrative techniques of creative nonfiction and is "lyrical." It is a moment, a singular instance of insight into human experience for the purpose of sharing an experience and revealing a deeper story truth.

The positive response to my "Call for Contributions" was overwhelming. People expressed a desire to share their stories, as storytelling is in our human nature to do so. I ended up receiving essays from 30 authors who expressed gratitude for being given the chance to reflect on the past which they found emotionally fulfilling and, indeed, cathartic. The book became my passion project, and it consumed my time for months as I wrote my own stories, collaborated with the authors on editing their work, and worked on putting together the anthology.

What the Objectives/Goals of This Book Are

Growing Up in an Immigrant Household and Community: Essays by Descendants of Immigrants is an anthology of personal and memoir essays that aims to accomplish several objectives/goals:

For the contributing authors:

- To have a voice and tell their stories of growing up in an immigrant household and community;
- To give voice, by extension, to their immigrant parents and grandparents.

For the readers:

- To be moved through an insightful look into the immigrant world;
- To relate to, empathize, and learn from other people's stories;
- To promote an understanding, acceptance, and validation of the experiences of immigrants;
- To promote an understanding, acceptance, and validation of the experiences of the descendants of immigrants and what they may go through to straddle both worlds—the immigrant and American cultures.

The intent is for this book to be like a bunch of stories that we, the children of immigrants, would be telling each other, say, sitting around a coffee table. We would share stories about how we perceived our parents or grandparents growing up—as hardworking, wise, weird, crazy, funny, overbearing, strict, or all of the above—and their immigrant ways—as strange, amusing, valuable, life-changing, or whatever— smiling, laughing, or crying while reminiscing.

America has the largest immigrant population in the world (Camarota & Zeigler, 2022). According to the U.S. Census Bureau, in 2023, 14.6 percent of the population was foreign-born. Immigrants form the fabric of our society, and the children of immigrants continue weaving that rich fabric. They enrich our communities and make our country unique and special. Their stories can teach us a lot about other cultures, including our own, and thus have compassion for the immigrant experience. By sharing their stories, this book hopes to advocate for immigration and multiculturalism to be celebrated, championed, and supported by our society.

We hope the stories resonate with immigrant families but also with young people who feel out of place or in the middle of two cultures and want to fit in somewhere. It is for people who, at some point in their lives, felt like "the other" or wanted to be accepted despite how different they or their parents were.

References

Bousquin, M. (2015, March 10). *Flash memoir: The benefits of writing short memoir.* Writing Women's Lives Academy. https://writingwomenslives.com/flash-memoir-benefits-writing-short-memoir/

Camarota, S. A., & Zeigler, K. (2022, October 27). Foreign-born population hits nearly 48 million in September 2022. Center for Immigration Studies. https://cis.org/Report/ForeignBorn-Population-Hits-Nearly-48-Million-September-2022

Nichols, M. (2015, January 20). *What's a flash essay?* Talking Writing: Creating Meaning through Personal Stories. https://talkingwriting.com/whats-flash-essay

How the Book Is Organized and What Each Section Is About

The book is organized into five sections, and each section focuses on a particular theme: (1) Challenges and Hardships; (2) Fond Childhood Memories of the Immigrant Community; (3) The Immigrant Household and Food; (4) Life Lessons Learned from Immigrant Parents; and (5) Life Lessons Learned from Immigrant Grandparents. The essays are grouped based on the predominant focus, although there is an overlap in themes. As such, some essays could easily fit into more than one section. After every title, I have added the ethnic background[1] in brackets. In my essay, which precedes the sections, I write about moving around as a child and having to adjust to new cultures which forced me to reflect and work on defining my cultural identity.

SECTION 1: CHALLENGES AND HARDSHIPS

This section focuses on the challenges and hardships that many descendants of immigrants face as a result of their ethnic and diverse heritage. Aida Zilelian in her essay "On Being Armenian," writes about how she felt growing up as a first-generation Armenian and the challenges that came with hailing from a country whose history is not understood or acknowledged by many people. In her riveting essay, "It Didn't Have to Be This Way: The Consequences of Strict Immigrant Parents," Patricia Lozano Miller describes her own horror being raised by strict Colombian parents who, while well-intentioned, made choices that had damaging consequences on her life. In her essay "*Il Dolce* (The Sweet)," Milena Scalzo, whose first language was Italian, looks back on a negative incident in school that made her feel different from her peers but that eventually had a significant influence on her career choice. Choices is what Alfredo Vinci's powerful essay "Save, Save, Save" is also about; Vinci discusses his Italian parents' penchant for saving and being economical, a well-known trait of many immigrants, but one that cost him a more comfortable life as an adult.

Comfortable is the opposite of how one feels when spelling out their long ethnic name or listening to someone else pronounce it. In his essay "Alphabet," Terry Stratoudakis recounts the seeming challenges but also actual benefits of having an ethnic name, his own covering most letters of the Greek and English alphabets. Like Terry, Nazli Diba also felt ambivalent about her name growing up as she writes, in her essay "Garlic," about how cultural differences in terms of food, language, and clothes set her apart from her American peers but also instilled in her a strong sense of self. In her essay "Distant Memories," our student author, Polina Oleynikova, also writes about the challenging but rewarding experiences of adjusting to American life as a daughter of Uzbek parents.

---

1. The common term *Greek* is used throughout the book to mean *Hellenic*.

SECTION 2: FOND CHILDHOOD MEMORIES OF THE IMMIGRANT COMMUNITY

This section is about fond childhood memories growing up in an immigrant community. In the essay "Authentic Trilingual NYC Upbringing and Immersion into Sicilian Roots," Silvia Rosselli Davi writes about her trilingual upbringing in Astoria, New York defined by her immersion into her father's Sicilian roots and her mother's Mexican heritage. In her essay "Treasure Island, the Bronx," Jean Ende takes us into a different borough, her aunt Gussy and uncle Harry's home in the Bronx, which was full of treasures and revelations of the America she lived in versus the "real" America.

The essay "My Birthday" is written from the perspective of my young self where I describe my 5th birthday party that takes place in our tiny apartment in Astoria, New York. The theme of fond childhood memories continues in Joy Scantlebury's essay, "Bajan Memories: Always in My Heart," which is about spending Christmas with her family and loved ones in White Plains, New York, infused with Bajan holiday traditions. Nadia Giannopoulos, in her essay "Summers in Greece," writes about a typical Greek tradition—spending summers in Greece—that taught her to value and appreciate family and the simple moments in life.

SECTION 3: THE IMMIGRANT HOUSEHOLD AND FOOD

This section focuses on the food in the immigrant household. My essay "Mamma Dina: Food as Love" is a tribute to my Greek mother, an exemplary cook whose passion for food and feeding people stemmed from her deprived upbringing and tough life. In her memoir essay "The Culinary Cardinal," Maria C. Palmer writes about her experiences, as a child, watching her Italian grandmother cook, and years later, as an adult, noticing a special visitor's appearance when she would try to recreate her nanna's recipes. Food means love, devotion, and family, and this is also evident in Cindy Li's essay about rice balls and her Taiwanese family ("Rice Ball Stick Together"). In her essay "First-Generation Persian-Jewish-American Family Thanksgivings and Blessings," Rebecca Yousefzadeh Sassouni gives us a taste of a Persian-Jewish-American Thanksgiving and the many blessings that the traditional holiday brings.

SECTION 4: LIFE LESSONS LEARNED FROM IMMIGRANT PARENTS

This section is about life lessons learned from immigrant parents. In her essay "A Letter of Gratitude", Maggie Blair writes a letter to her parents, thanking them for teaching her the values of education, faith, personal growth, and professional success. Gloria Serwa Gyimah, in her essay "The Values Instilled in Me by My Parents," discusses the work ethic and perseverance that her parents instilled in her. Like Gloria's parents, Fiffy Eliades's parents were also role models who sacrificed so much for their family and who, unfortunately, lost their lives prematurely, as she discusses in her essay "My Parents' Ultimate Sacrifice."

A few authors decided to write about the special role that their immigrant mothers have played in their lives. Noreen Williams in her essay "Practicality" discusses the challenging relationship that she and her Irish mother had when she was a teenager, one that eventually taught her valuable lessons of practicality and independence. In the essay "Ode to Glendita," Ashley Tavormina writes an ode to her strong and inspiring Honduran mother who had to raise her children without a father. Mubina Schroeder, in the essay "Better than a Thousand Sons," documents her feelings of being raised by her special Indian/Pakistani mother, a positive force in her life, and of losing her to a terrible illness. In her essay "Guidance from a Guyanese Mother", Nadia Khan-Roopnarine writes about a few interesting Guyanese superstitions that her mother passed down to her and that she now passes down to her own children. In the essay "Mother and Children Discuss Immigrant Experiences," Sherone Smith-Sánchez takes a unique approach and presents a letter exchange in which her four children share their perspectives of growing up in their Jamaican mother's household and her response to their letters.

SECTION 5: LIFE LESSONS LEARNED FROM IMMIGRANT GRANDPARENTS

This section centers on life lessons learned from immigrant grandparents. In the essay "Opposites Attract," Joanne O'Brien pays tribute to her Irish and Croatian grandparents who taught her courage and generosity. Likewise, in the essay "My Immigrant Grandparents," Rickey Moroney is thankful to her European grandparents for shaping her into the person she is today. Peggy Pyrovolakis, in her essay "Greek Women in the Family," writes about the powerful Greek women in her life who taught her strength and love. In her essay "*Yiayia*," Matina Stergiopoulos writes about her charming grandmother who would often give her lessons about the opportunities that the American Dream afforded her.

Like grandmothers, grandfathers also have a special place in the heart of many, and without exception, Tim Roda's Italian grandfather taught him to hustle and strive to be successful ("The Immigrant Hustle"). In the essay "My Grandfather, the Legend," our student author and my oldest son, Emanuel Giouroukakis (16 years old), recounts the legendary reputation of his late Greek paternal grandfather whom he never met. Our other student author and my youngest son, Paul Giouroukakis (12 years old), in his essay "Growing Up with a Pappou," recounts his fond memories of growing up with his Greek maternal grandfather who taught him the values of hard work and family.

What the Reader Should Expect

Although there are thousands of media sources that relate the trials and tribulations of immigrants coming to this country to pursue the American Dream, there are few that document the experiences of children of immigrants who typically straddle two worlds, the world of their parents, and the country in which they are born.

Growing Up in an Immigrant Household and Community: Essays by Descendants of Immigrants is a collection of essays that aims to give a voice to descendants of immigrants (individuals born in the United States to immigrant parents or grandparents) by sharing their stories of what it was like growing up in an immigrant household and community, and how these experiences influenced the development of their identity.

When you read the essays in this book, you will be amazed at how similar they are, despite the diversity in topic, content, culture, voice, tone, language, and so on. They are similar because of the common themes inherent in the immigrant experience (i.e., challenges/hardships; fond childhood memories of traditions, celebrations, pastime; food and family; and life lessons learned, like hard work and perseverance) but also because they evoke common emotions, like joy, anger, sadness, and love.

These folks are from all walks of life (they differ in terms of age, ethnicity, culture, background, education, employment, and experiences). Some contributing authors are published; three are secondary school students; for others, this is the first attempt at writing a piece for publication. Yet, in this collection, the authors come together to tell their intriguing and poignant stories of adversity, good times, and lessons learned from growing up in an immigrant household and community. In coming together, we have created our own *family* united by our common experiences.

The strength of these essays is twofold: They are authentic, and they are written from the heart. They will move you, make you feel any number of emotions (e.g., joy, contentment, amusement, sadness, disappointment, anger, nostalgia), and perhaps even change you. We hope you will be able to relate to, understand, or empathize with the themes, events, or characters in these stories.

We invite you to become a part of this storytelling and, as you are reading each essay, think about your own upbringing and how your cultural experiences have defined your identity.

Editor's Essay

EXCERPT

Growing up the daughter of immigrant parents is like straddling two worlds, the world of my parents and the world I was born in. When I am in Greece, I am considered an American. In America, I am a Greek. I live in both worlds without second thought because that is what bicultural people do. Being born or raised in more than one culture, even though a privilege, adds another layer to a person's search for their identity.

The author in her elementary-school classroom in Greece

The author with her husband, John, and children (from left to right, Emanuel, Paul, and Anna) in front of their house in Chania, Crete in 2019

The author's parents—from left to right, mother-in-law, Anna, father Polychronis, and late mother, Constantina

The author's late mother, Constantina, and grandmother, Vasiliki

Ditmars Boulevard and 31st Street in Astoria, Queens, New York

Source: https://forgotten-ny.com/2012/01/north-astoria-queens/

Straddling Two Worlds: Defining My Greek-American Identity

[Greek]

Vicky Giouroukakis

Growing up the daughter of immigrant parents is like straddling two worlds, the world of my parents and the world in which I was born. When I am in Greece, I am considered an American. In America, I am a Greek. I live in both worlds without second thought because that is what bicultural people do. Being born or raised in more than one culture, even though a privilege, adds another layer to a person's search for their identity.

Growing Up in a Greek American Community

1980. I am seven years old and walking down Ditmars Boulevard in Astoria, New York. I pass by the local restaurants, coffee shops, and fruit stalls. There are Greek store signs everywhere—Thessaloniki Jewelers, Vangeli's Bakaliko, John's Barber Shop, and Mike's Diner. I know these stores evoke a feeling of nostalgia for my parents. I smell the fresh bread outside of LaGuli Pastry Shop and the irresistible waft of grilled meat from the souvlaki cart on the corner. I hear the Greek language spoken everywhere, which I know makes people who speak little English, like my parents, feel comfortable. Mr. Vangeli, the owner of the Greek deli, sees me and runs outside in his white apron to tell me he got in the imported feta my mom had wanted. Through the glass window of Atlantic Bank, I see Carmelo, the security guard, waving at me. He is always so kind to my mother whenever she comes to the bank and asks to be directed to the right teller who can help her.

My childhood in the Greek American town of Astoria was a happy one and had the best of both worlds. Like other immigrants, my parents, Polychronis and Constantina, moved there in 1969 in pursuit of work, a better life, and a sense of community. They were fortunate to be in the land of opportunity after witnessing war and famine in Greece following the German occupation. Their fathers both died when my parents were young, so to support their families they worked on the farm and then in various jobs in Athens. They barely finished elementary school because they could not afford to continue, but they were smart, hardworking, and determined to succeed. In Astoria, mom got a job at the Bulova Watch Factory where she meticulously assembled watches. She was proud and grateful that she had secured such a high-paying job with limited English proficiency. Dad worked at our local pizzeria, Pizza Palace, and years later owned his own gyro restaurant near Fordham University in the Bronx. He worked 12-hour days, 7 days a week but always came home with a smile on his face.

It was important for my parents to maintain our Greek identity and instill in my two brothers, Steve and George, and me a pride for our heritage. Therefore, they did everything possible to keep our family close to the Greek community, and thereby closer to them. The Greek culture, religion, and language were maintained through the churches. As such, we attended liturgy and religious instruction at St. Catherine's Greek Orthodox Church every Sunday. My parents believed in the power of prayer and thanked God every day, in both good and bad moments, for their good fortune and would say at times, "God has enough for everyone." They taught us to be good and humble people and warned us against excessive pride.

Housed in the church was our private, parochial school where my Greek American peers and I were taught the main subjects in English but also Greek language, history, religion, and culture. We wore uniforms and often went through checks for lice, dirty nails, and, for the boys, prohibited long hair. We celebrated and had assemblies for the Greek national holidays that included traditional Greek dancing. The lunch we brought from home consisted of Greek staples—pastitsio, lentils, and spaghetti and meat sauce—and the occasional baloney sandwich.

Many of our Astorian neighbors became our friends and our substitute family. My siblings and I played in the street with the other kids in the neighborhood until dusk. We played chase, jump rope, hopscotch, and hide-and-seek. My best friend, Toula, and I would roller-skate leisurely or race with great speed whenever it struck our fancy. Our resources were few, so we played with what we had. I remember building small houses out of carton boxes and pretending they were our homes. Helen, another friend, would take the lead on this as she was older and had good motor skills. During breaks, she ate slices of watermelon with the rind to the disgust of us younger ones. We played board games that we drew with chalk on the street and used bottle caps stuffed with Play-Doh as pawns.

We spoke Greek at home and English with our friends. We knew everyone on the block, and they knew us, what parts of Greece my parents were from, where they worked, how many kids they had, and our ages and personalities. Everyone's circumstances were the same. We were working-class, immigrant families striving to make a living.

Our American friends might have thought our Greek traditions, superstitions, and idiosyncrasies were strange. We always wore the evil eye to ward off negative spells. At Easter, we roasted lamb as a representation of Jesus's sacrifice. Even the way we did our cross in church was different from the Catholic way. At home, we had at hand a *kerasma* (treat) at all times in case guests came by which was a part of our *philoxenia* (hospitality); guests were expected to take the food and drink so as not to offend. We had parties where we broke plates for good luck, and, if there was a band, threw dollar bills at the dancers. There were no sleepovers, and curfew was strict and inflexible. Our conversations were always loud and animated, as we love to argue for the sake of arguing. And pathos imbued everything we did. Remember Zorba the Greek?

Growing up in a working-class family made me envious of upper-class parents. Why did my parents always have to count every penny and save money? Why did they have to work long hours? Why was I left at friends' homes as a kid when my parents had to work late? Why couldn't I get the Barbie doll I longed for at age 7 and the big grand piano I would constantly ask for at age 11? Why couldn't dad be more like my friend's dad, who was a banker and occasionally lunched with his daughters to discuss current events? Why couldn't we go to restaurants or plays? Why couldn't we go on vacation to other places besides Greece?

As I matured, I learned that my parents gave me the best gift in life—a good work ethic—and the humble upbringing made me appreciate the value of things, the beauty of life, and the goodness in people.

Moving to Athens, Greece in Third Grade

1981. I am 8 years old. Amerikana (American Girl)! Amerikana! The sound pierces through the wind and reaches my ears. I look in the direction from where it came and see my classmates, all 15 of them, playing in the playground of our Athenian elementary school, and there is Anna looking at me exasperated—perhaps because I did not turn around sooner—and I wonder, Oh, Anna is calling ME, *I realize.*

The pendulum swung toward the Greek side when my parents moved the family to a working-class neighborhood in Athens, Greece, where I enrolled in third grade in our local public school. My classmates called me "Amerikana," and even though the name set me apart, it made me proud to be unique. I looked and dressed differently and was fluent in English and Greek. I was blonde and blue-eyed in a sea of classmates with primarily dark features, and I wore clothes of American brands that I had bought in the states. The school was different from the parochial school I had attended. Schedules were staggering, and so there were morning sessions and afternoon sessions to accommodate all the students. We also went home for lunch. Bathrooms in the school had squat toilets and were certainly not what I was used to in the States. After every class period, there was a 10-minute break for rest, snack, or play with our peers in the playground. We exercised during gym class and after school, when we prepared for track-and-field competitions, which took place at a major stadium in Athens.

Despite the initial culture shock I experienced in my new environment, I fully assimilated to the Greek education system and culture. In school, I became a top student and was consistently selected to act in the school performances. I attended British language school in the evenings to brush up on my English, which gave me a new appreciation for the language. My peers became my best friends when I longed for my friends in America and nurtured my desire to just be an ordinary kid, like them, even though the move had already pushed me into maturity.

In Athens, we lived a typical (Greek) life that was different from our life in the States. We lived in an apartment that was still too small to accommodate our family but much bigger than the one in Astoria. The tenants of our building shared the same culture and values. We were fortunate to have my dad home more often, since he had a more normal schedule working at the dry-cleaning department of the Marriott hotel in Athens. He eventually rose to a managerial position to the pride of our family. We had parties and invited relatives we had not seen in years.

My closest friends were my classmates and kids in the neighborhood who enjoyed exploring nature and climbing the hill behind our house. The weather was always mild, and it almost never snowed in Athens, so we were outdoors most of the times. We dug the earth for gold and picked wildflowers in the spring. We lived close to a park with swings that became our second home and where we met and befriended a stray golden retriever who would follow us everywhere.

Unlike in Astoria, we went to the farmers market for fresh food twice a week and the local bakery for hot-out-of-the-oven peasant's bread every morning. Every Saturday in the summer, we could hear the loud voice on the speaker coming from the itinerant grocery truck making its rounds in our neighborhood: "Freska karpouzia kai peponia!" (fresh watermelon and melon!).

A Greek home would be remiss without the presence of a grandma. Grandma Vasiliki (my namesake) came to live with us when my father started traveling to New York on business. Mom would often visit him, and so my grandmother moved in to care for her grandchildren as all Greek grandmothers are known to do. Grandma had long, silky blonde-white hair that she put up in a bun. She was widowed when she was very young and since then had always wore a black dress—it was typical for Greeks who lost loved ones to wear black as a sign of mourning. She was strong and healthy but always complained about her back and asked for heat patches to alleviate the pain. At night in bed when trying to put me to sleep, grandma would tell me stories, adapted versions of Cinderella and Little Red Riding Hood. She would often relate Cinderella to her life as she also grew up with a mean stepmother who mistreated her. Perhaps her storytelling inspired me to read and write stories when I got older.

Grandma Vasiliki was nurturing, kind, understanding, and strict but lenient when necessary. She cooked my favorite meal—fried pork chops; I still can't eat them without being reminded of her. She never opened the door to strangers, climbed four flights of stairs when alone for fear of getting stuck inside the elevator, locked the balcony doors, and went out only to the bakery, while my older brother, Steve, did the major shopping at the supermarket. Grandma Vasiliki could not read or write. Despite her lack of education, it was her maternal instinct that helped her raise us and survive life in the big city.

Moving Back to Astoria, New York in Eighth Grade

1986. I am 13 years old. The first day I walk into my first-period class, I see the same friends I had in second grade before I left for Greece, yet I feel different. My clothes are different, I am not wearing any makeup, and I feel self-conscious. I start speaking Greek (fluently and with a native accent) to my Greek teacher, and her mouth drops. She smiles and asks me about life in Greece. We talk for a while, and I look around to my classmates whom I feel are staring at me. Do they see me, or do I see myself as the fresh off-the-boat Greek?

Moving back to the States and entering middle school at the tender age of 13 shifted the pendulum toward the American side. The impetus for the move was twofold: my father's business opportunity and my brother's enrollment in a college in New York. Leaving Greece was a shock to my system and made me resent my parents for a long time. The experience of entering middle school as a new student from another country was both difficult and profoundly life-changing. I had changed and was not the same person, so I felt that I could not relate to my peers. I was literate in Greek and ahead in math, and I still followed contemporary Greek politics, art, and music. I could identify with my Greek culture to a greater degree than my classmates and befriended a couple of like-minded, American-born students from Greece who had also experienced a cultural shift.

Freedom to explore non-Greek friendships came when I enrolled in a public high school in eleventh grade. My parents pleaded with me to stay in the safe environment of the parochial school but eventually relented to my persistent arguments. In this new environment, I felt more acculturated into American society and more confident. I befriended a diverse group of kids and joined multiple school clubs. I was given opportunities to excel and received scholarships (and financial aid) which helped alleviate the financial burden on my family.

Applying to college as a first-generation American is like driving blind—you don't know where the car will take you, but you trust it enough to take you there safely. When I was applying to college, I didn't know much about most colleges, and I didn't have a network of resources, tutors, college advisors, or even tuition money. All I had were my parents' support and hard work ethic, and my own drive to receive an education and succeed.

My parents deeply believed in education as the means to a successful life. I applied on my own to big-name colleges because of their reputations. I ended up at Ivy League schools and worked harder than most people, since I had to navigate the world of academia without many resources. My parents were not educated to give me advice about how to succeed in academia—the need for networking, how to make connections, how to promote yourself, and how to use professors as contacts to seek employment.

Fortunately, I had caring professors who became my mentors and helped me succeed. My parents had no idea what I was majoring in or why I was spending so many years in school ("A master's in English education, a doctorate in literacy education? What is that?"). In my 10-year, postsecondary schooling, I even "snuck in" a second master's degree, this one in teaching English to nonnative speakers because I empathized with their challenges. Despite their lack of full understanding of my degrees and career choice, my parents provided me with unrequited support.

At the universities I attended, I joined their Hellenic clubs to connect with the Greek element. Being in NYC with a large Greek population, it was not difficult to do that. At NYU, there were even two Hellenic student associations, one for Greek American students and the other for students from Greece. I was split between them and didn't know which one to join, so I participated in both. At the time, Columbia also had an influx of international students from Greece, which made its Hellenic club lively. The University of Pennsylvania did not have a club, so I started one that other graduate students took over after I left. I never missed marching in the annual parade, whether in Philadelphia or New York, that celebrates the Greek declaration of independence from the Ottoman Empire on March 25, 1821.

Looking back as an adult, I realize that moving around a lot and being forced to adapt to new environments—whether a new country, school, or higher education institution—helped me grow up faster and become more resilient and adaptable to change.

Growing Up Bilingual

1986. I am watching the show, "Full House," on cable television in our living room with my friend. My father walks in the room and greets my friend:

Hi, Tina. How are you? Everything good?

He turns to me and says, "Vicky, ela na mou peis ti leei afto to gramma apo to Con Edison" (Vicky, come tell me what this letter from Con Edison says).

I turn around and respond in Greek:

"Nai, tha to kano. Later, though, OK?" (Yes, I will. Later, though, OK?)

My father nods and leaves the room. I turn to my friend and remind her in English that one of the main actors on the show, John Stamos, is of Greek descent.

Growing up bilingual meant I had to straddle two linguistic worlds and be prepared to alternate languages when the situation arose. Code-switching was constant, as we used both languages simultaneously to communicate more effectively. Switching languages is like playing an instrument to one tune and singing a different tune at the same time but still producing a coherent piece of music. You vary the music as the context changes and you take into consideration the purpose, who the listener is, and how you want to communicate your message. You make quick decisions on the spot.

When I was younger, I would cringe when my parents addressed me in Greek or broken English. They mispronounced common words, like "baco" for "bagel" and "tsiken" for "chicken" They used the infamous Greekglish, made-up words, which has become material for jokes (e.g., "mapa" for mop and "movaro" for "move"). Well into my teenage years, I discovered the value of using Greek as a secret language. It came in handy when I didn't want my American friends to understand what my parents and I were saying during car rides.

Being fluent in both languages meant I had a responsibility to act as an interpreter for my parents. Translating for them was a burden during my adolescent and young adult life—reading their mail, settling utility matters with the electric and gas companies, and visiting doctors and social security agencies—not because I was obliged to do it, but because my parents would get upset if they didn't understand my explanations. That has not changed to this day.

Today, I am thankful for being raised bilingual. Bilingual or multilingual people are said to have "language smarts" because they need to make swift decisions as to which language to use in every situation. Beyond the cognitive benefits, multilinguals have academic, economic, and social advantages that are necessary for success in career and life. However, multilingualism can also be a source of frustration for many who at some point in their lives may experience a sense of being in limbo or caught between two languages. They know they need to use the dominant language but may want or need to draw from their other languages as resources to communicate more effectively. Code-switching is another part of the identity of multilinguals who use several languages in their everyday contexts and try to make sense of their complex lives and worlds. To this day, I enjoy every opportunity to use the Greek language.

All Grown Up: A Defined Greek American Identity

1993. I am 20 years old and vacationing in Athens with my friend Dora and we are having a drink at a local coffee shop. Dora sees her cousin, beckons him to come over, and she proceeds to introduce me to her cousin as her friend from America. Her friend starts speaking to me in English in a thick accent. I reply in fluent Greek, and he is amazed. "Ah, you speak Greek! But you don't look Greek," he says. I am used to such a reaction, but I do not understand it. What does a Greek person look like anyway? Even though I want desperately to fit in more fully with natives—after all, I am fluent in Greek, I lived and was educated in Greece, I am familiar with Greek culture, and I feel Greek—I am still perceived as a foreigner, a Greek of the diaspora.

It wasn't until my mid-20s that I realized and came to accept that my identity is not one or the other—Greek or American—but rather both. In the diaspora literature, there is a term for an ethnic identity that experts call binational or transnational Greekness.

> Unlike the assimilationist Greek American, the binational Greek actively cultivates the culture of the ancestral homeland, but unlike the diaspora American Greek, the binational Greek simultaneously embraces the culture of the new world. Instead of agonizing over the choice between two cultures, resisting and even resenting the language of one or the other, binationals are comfortable with both.[2]

Transnationalism helps connect people across borders and allows for globalization and cultural understanding. By coming together, we learn about new ideas, values, belief systems, cuisines, and ways of communicating and expressing ourselves. We celebrate and validate our own and other cultures. We become aware of our similarities and differences which helps us understand that our humanity is the common thread that binds us.

Transnationalism goes hand in hand with translanguaging. Translanguaging maintains that the multilingual mind is a complete and active system of linguistic resources that are used for different communicative functions. In the field of education, where translanguaging is used as an approach, students are encouraged to use both languages in class, one language strengthening the other, to facilitate understanding of subject matter. This code-switching has enormous benefits for students that include the potential to enhance students' academic and personal growth as well as their sense of identity.

Perhaps my parents became transnationalists in their lifetimes as they embraced both the traditional Greek views of women but also modern American views. They expect dating to be serious and to lead to marriage, which is the only way to move out of your parents' house. A woman should learn to cook and clean, keep a good household, and raise children. Yet, according to my mother, a woman also has to be strong, independent, and self-reliant.

---

2. Dan Georgakas, director of the Greek American Studies Project of the Center for Byzantine and Modern Greek Studies at Queens College, CUNY, presented the second annual Dr. Dimitri and Irmgard Pallas Lecture in Modern Greek Studies. An expanded version of the lecture appeared in the *Journal of Modern Hellenism*, 21-22, Winter 2004-5.

Having a career is also important to my parents, which was demonstrated when they helped raise my own kids so that I could work.

It is no surprise, then, that family put pressure on me to marry at a child-bearing age. Marrying a Greek was a necessity in most Greek families, a wish in some, and a choice for me. I knew that even after dating people of different faiths and ethnicities, my dream would be to marry a Greek, which I did, not so much to please my parents as to make myself happy given how much I identify with my heritage. John and I had a big wedding with 350 guests which was a grand family affair. Have you seen the movie, *My Big Fat Greek Wedding*? We invited relatives and friends on both sides with the help of our parents who made sure nobody was left off the guest list who would be offended. We were particular about having a rich abundance of food, as not having enough at a Greek wedding is cause for gossip. The band played all types of music, including Greek and Cretan to honor John's side of the family, and we danced for hours.

While I consider myself an American, I also embrace my Greek heritage. I taught English at the public high school that I attended and was the advisor of the Hellenic club. At the university where I now teach future teachers, I also serve as advisor of its Hellenic club. I mentor young people and try to raise awareness of Greek history and culture. In my local church, I have been involved in activities that include counseling youth on career matters, volunteering at the food booth of the annual festival, coordinating fundraising activities, and serving in multiple roles at the Greek language afternoon school.

As a parent, I try to raise my three children—Emanuel, Anna, and Paul—to be bilingual and bicultural. They are proud of America's rich history, founding principles, democracy and freedom, opportunities to achieve success, and sports (they are fanatical football, hockey, lacrosse, and soccer fans). My children are also proud of their Greek heritage and Greek-Orthodox faith. They attended our church's Greek language afternoon school for 10 years and have been participating in the church's young association. My two oldest restarted the Greek club at their high school to promote an awareness of Greek history and culture. As a family, we try to honor the traditions and rituals of Greece as best we can and vacation every year in Greece where we have a home.

Straddling multiple worlds and finding the right balance is key to achieving contentment, but it can be challenging. It is my hope that multinationals and multicultural people can explore their identity, appreciate their multiple cultures, and find solace in who they are without struggling to belong to any one world.

Challenges and Hardships

On Being Armenian 3
   [Armenian]
   Aida Zilelian

It Didn't Have to Be This Way: The Consequences of Strict Immigrant Parents 7
   [Colombian]
   Patricia Lozano Miller

***Il Dolce* (The Sweet)** 11
   [Italian]
   Milena Perna Scalzo

Save, Save, Save 14
   [Italian]
   Alfredo Vinci

Alphabet 17
   [Greek]
   Terry Stratoudakis

Garlic 21
   [Persian]
   Nazli Diba

Distant Memories 24
   [Uzbek] [Student Essay]
   Polina Oleynikova

Aida Zilelian

Aida Zilelian is a first-generation, American-Armenian writer, educator, and storyteller from Queens, NY. Her debut novel *The Legacy of Lost Things* was published in 2015 and was the recipient of the 2014 Tololyan Literary Award. Aida has been featured on NPR, *The Huffington Post*, *Kirkus Reviews*, *Poets & Writers Magazine*, and various reading series throughout Queens and Manhattan. She is also the curator of Boundless Tales, which was one of the longest running reading series in Queens, NY. Her short story collection *These Hills Were Meant for You* was shortlisted for the 2018 Katherine Anne Porter Award. Aida's most recent novel, *All the Ways We Lied*, is forthcoming in January 2024 (Keylight Books). She is currently working on completing her short story collection, *Where There Can Be No Breath at All*.

The author

EXCERPT

Adding to my hollow sense of identity was another layer that would alienate me from my peers: I was a first-generation Armenian. To a passive onlooker, this would not mean all that much. But to me, it meant being deprived of joys that felt significant.

On Being Armenian

[Armenian]

Aida Zilelian

I was in my seventh grade social studies class, and we had just completed a geography unit on Europe and the Middle East. I was sitting in my usual seat in the back row listening to my teacher, Mrs. Barone, talk about the coming events after the new year.

"We're going to have a cultural celebration," she explained, "and I will be asking each of you to bring in a dish from your country of origin."

I noted the date and decided I would feign illness the night before.

"Now let's go around the room and share our country of origin, even if your parents are third or fourth generation."

I watched as my classmates stood up one by one. Italy. Germany. Russia. Israel. Korea. When it was my turn, I stood up and mumbled, "Armenia."

"You have to speak up, Aida. We can't hear you from all the way in the back."

It wouldn't have made a difference if I had said it through a loudspeaker. "Armenia."

My classmates looked at each other wonderingly, as if I had created a mythical land. They snickered. I heard one of them say, "Arma—who?"

It was the same face they made when I unpacked my lunch in the cafeteria, where I endured their imaginative and crude speculations of what I was eating.

"What *is* that?" someone had once asked, conveying the table's collective revulsion.

"Dolma," I had said.

I had looked down at the meat-stuffed zucchini covered in garlicky yogurt and sumac, realizing the question was more a declaration of disgust.

The anonymity of my origin followed me everywhere. Most adults had never heard of Armenia.

"Alba*ni*an?" someone once asked.

"No," I said. "Armenian."

"Where is that?"

Patiently, I would explain that we were part of the Soviet Republic. I wanted to tell them that historically, we were the first people to accept Christianity as a religion; that our first churches were built in the 4th century; and that the Genocide in 1915 had orphaned my grandfather, and my father's side of the family consisted of my grandmother, my aunt, and my father. When I peered at the map hanging in my bedroom I saw the small speck of land, the size of a fingernail bordered in the center of Turkey, Iran, and Azerbaijan. We wouldn't claim independence until 1991.

"Don't forget that you are a Zilelian!" my father would say.

He was practically fanatical, his obsession with our family name and Armenian heritage. For me who felt invisible by the world, his emphatic stance seemed overblown and embarrassing.

Worse still was explaining to people the turn of the century Genocide during World War I and the Turkish government's denial of murdering nearly two-million Armenians. If no one knew what Armenia was, how would this crime against humanity, against my people ever be recognized? I did not feel marginalized, overlooked, or discriminated against; I felt as if I did not exist.

I looked through books about the Genocide that my father had purchased from the Armenian Prelacy, turning each page over with the realization that my father's aunts, uncles, and relatives had all been killed. Pictures of the barren Syrian desert and a long procession of Armenians on a death march. Disembodied heads placed on shelves as if on display. Skeletal bodies in a heaping pile in a mass grave. Images of the front pages of *The New York Times*: "Million Armenians Killed or In Exile, Armenians Sent to Perish in Desert"—it would all plague me. The world had looked on silently and done nothing. And nearly 100 years later, it seemed no one knew who we were, who I was.

Adding to my hollow sense of identity was another layer that would alienate me from my peers: I was a first-generation Armenian. To a passive onlooker, this would not mean all that much. But to me, it meant being deprived of joys that felt significant. That I did not go trick-or-treating: "I'm not sending you to strangers' homes begging for candy." There were no sleepovers: "You have your own bed to sleep in. You don't need to sleep anywhere else." I was discouraged from having American friends: "You can play with your sister and your cousins" (who all lived out of state).

Their goal was not to isolate me anymore than I already was, but to protect me from a fate that was equivalent to death: marrying an *odar*—an American. Ironically, the word means out of place, unfamiliar. And it's the feeling that consumed me for most of my upbringing. Looking back, I wonder if my parents realized the naivete of their expectations. I attended Armenian elementary school five days a week, followed by Armenian Saturday school and Sunday school at the Armenian church in Manhattan. I didn't realize it then, but I was suffocating.

Looking back, there were glimmers of happiness that I experienced. The Festival of Grapes, which was held annually in Astoria's Bohemian Hall: There, we all came together and danced, ate, ran around with friends as Armenian music blared through the speakers.

The *bara-hanteses* (dinner dances) were a splendid thing. Platters of food crowding our dinner table, the noise and chatter of people speaking Armenian, the live band bringing to life the albums my parents played on Sunday afternoons. We were a clan, orphaned by tragedy.

It wasn't until years after my parents' scandalous divorce and remarrying that I was able to break away from my community. I married an American and had one child. I wrote a novel that received an award funded by an Armenian foundation. At my book signing, I stood in awe at the sight of all the Armenians, many of whom I did not know personally, who had come to support me. They were there because I was one of them. They didn't need to know me. I remember their beaming faces sitting in the crowd and how proud they seemed that an Armenian had written a book and it was being celebrated.

After the event, many of them approached me to extend their congratulations. I was ashamed, suddenly, that I had turned away from my Armenian culture.

The distance of decades since my adolescence has come full circle in my realizations. I understand that I am part of an ancient history, a small and mighty tribe. And that we are not fragile. We defied the age-old cliché of reigning strength in numbers. What matters really is that we are still here.

Patricia Lozano Miller

Patricia Lozano Miller was born January 4, 1961, in Jackson Heights, Queens, NY to Colombian parents. She is the oldest of three children and the only member of her immediate family to graduate from college. She attended Stony Brook University and earned a bachelor's degree in liberal arts in 1988. Patricia worked a variety of jobs throughout her life, the most recent being a staff assistant in the Longwood Central School district where her two daughters attended. Today, she resides in Middle Island, NY with her husband John, daughters Danielle and Emily, and her future son-in-law Michael. She also spends most of her time with her dog Buddy and grand-puppy Breezy. She enjoys a simple life in the company of her loved ones.

The author with her parents, Hilda and Hernando Lozano, at her high school graduation in June 1979

EXCERPT

I remember feeling disappointed that my father was nothing like my friend Kelly's father. Kelly's father was easygoing. She was allowed to go on a trip to Florida with her cheerleading team that was accompanying the football team in elementary school, and there I was, not even sure if I would be given permission to go out with friends on a Friday night. When I reflected on my feelings of disappointment, I realized that the biggest difference between my dad and Kelly's dad was that my dad was an immigrant, and hers was not.

It Didn't Have to Be This Way: The Consequences of Strict Immigrant Parents

[Colombian]

Patricia Lozano Miller

Junior high school in the mid-1970s—what a fun time! I remember being around 13 years old when I wanted to join my friends at the school dances that took place every Friday night. There was a lot of excitement around my friends who were all busy making plans for the dance as to whose parents were going to drive whom and what time they would meet. It wasn't easy for my Colombian-born parents to accept that this was the cultural and social norm for their eldest teen daughter. I had to do chores around the house and needed to wait for my father to get home from work before I would even try to ask for his permission to go. My mother was home cooking dinner, but my father ruled the household with an iron fist, and his approval was what I was constantly after. When my father walked in the door after a hard day's work as a traffic manager, I couldn't approach him just yet. I knew that I had to wait until he finished his dinner before I could speak to him about the plans that I wanted to make. I remember the nerve-racking feelings of uncertainty while he ate his dinner, waiting and wondering if I would be allowed to join my friends. For these dances, he would almost always say yes, but I will never forget how he made me wait. He made sure I knew that he was the boss.

My father's strict rule became even more apparent as I went into high school. I recall a tenth grade ski trip that I wanted to go on. I asked for my parents' permission, which was really only my father's. He said no and didn't tell me why. There was no compromise; a second effort to get him to change his mind was pointless. I always felt like he didn't trust me. Around the same time, boys in my classes began to show interest in me and wanted to come over to my house. My father would make it very uncomfortable for any male friends that visited. They were not allowed to sit in his designated lounge chair. They could not go in my room, and immediately upon walking in, they needed to shake my father's hand and answer the question, "What are your intentions with my daughter?" which, looking back at now, seems to be way too serious of a question to be asking 15- and 16-year-old boys.

I remember feeling disappointed that my father was nothing like my friend Kelly's father. Kelly's father was easygoing. She was allowed to go on a trip to Florida with her cheerleading team that was accompanying the football team in elementary school, and there I was, not even sure if I would be given permission to go out with friends on a Friday night. When I reflected on my feelings of disappointment, I realized that the biggest difference between my dad and Kelly's dad was that my dad was an immigrant, and hers was not.

Both of my parents were not there for me emotionally. When we sat down around the dinner table we never spoke. We ate in silence. Nobody asked, "How was your day?" or "What's going on in your life?" I asked my friend Kelly if her family also ate dinner in silence. She said no, and I again found myself feeling disappointed that my family wasn't like Kelly's family.

After high school, I was caught up in the disco era. I used to go out dancing at the clubs with my friends on the weekends while still living at home going to a commuter college. There was one time when I came home in the early morning hours after a fun night out. The sun was just about rising when I stood at the front door, and as I began to open it, my father was standing there blocking the doorway. He wouldn't let me in. He stood there, in silence, with a look on his face that terrified me. He wasn't going to move. His disapproval for my staying out all night slapped me in the face. I found it disturbing that he didn't even express concern for my whereabouts but instead was quick to anger. The only place I could think to go to was my cousin's house. If anyone could understand what had just happened, it would be my cousin.

I began to resent my parents' strict nature and lack of understanding. I became rebellious—I didn't care about pleasing them anymore and was doing what I wanted. I invited my platonic male friend to sleep over against my father's will. I continued staying out late going to the disco and dating around, much to my parents' disapproval. My grades suffered, and as a result, I was academically dismissed from college. My parents, instead of making an effort to get to know me, decided that the best course of action for their rebellious 21-year-old daughter was to drop her off at a psychiatric hospital.

I sat in a room at the hospital with my mother, sister (with whom I was never close), and a counselor who tried to get a grasp on the situation. As the counselor facilitated a family session, I became extremely upset, angry, and frustrated with my mother and sister, who I felt were betraying me by saying I was unhinged and out of control. The anger that I felt provoked me and I ended up pushing my mother. I had deep-seated feelings of resentment and frustration. I wasn't unhinged or out of control but rather misunderstood by my immigrant parents.

Because I pushed my mother, I was deemed to be violent and admitted to the hospital. I felt so out of place. I lost all my friends, and I felt like there was no reason for me to be where I was. It was a nightmare. On the phone, I begged to come home, and my parents didn't want to hear it.

It took me many years and a lot of therapy to realize that this traumatic experience happened not because there was something wrong with me but because of the ignorance of my immigrant parents. They lacked the knowledge of American culture and tried too hard to contain and control me. When I reflect on my upbringing, I can't help but think that it didn't have to be so traumatic. If my parents made more of an effort to assimilate to American society, maybe they wouldn't have been so strict and rigid. It didn't have to be this way.

    I went on to finish my bachelor's degree and became the only member of my immediate family to graduate college. I didn't want to be uneducated like my mother. Later in my life, my father, who at this point was retired, apologized to me. His exact words were, "I'm sorry I was so hard on you. I didn't know what you were going through." Hearing those words from him lifted a weight from my shoulders. I forgave him because to forgive is to be forgiven. As I started my own family, my father became gentler, softer, and kinder. When I became a parent, I made it my mission not to be like my parents. One of the best things I have done as a parent has been trusting my children. I communicate with them and express my love for them often because I don't want them to experience the familial hardships that I did while growing up in an immigrant family.

Milena Scalzo

Milena Perna Scalzo is the daughter of Incoronata Garofalo and Filippo Perna who bravely left their small town in Italy after marriage to start a new life on Long Island, New York. Milena grew up in a traditional Italian family, speaking fluent Italian, and spending most summers in Italy with family. Milena was the first person in her family to attend college and receive a higher degree. Convincing Italian parents to allow her to study away at Siena College in Albany was quite a feat. Then, she attended Hofstra University for her master's degree. Milena is an educator at the North Shore School District, currently teaching third grade in this wonderful, creative community. She lives in Manhasset with her family who love to travel and experience new adventures. Milena loves to treat herself to a "dolce" but has little affection for the donut.

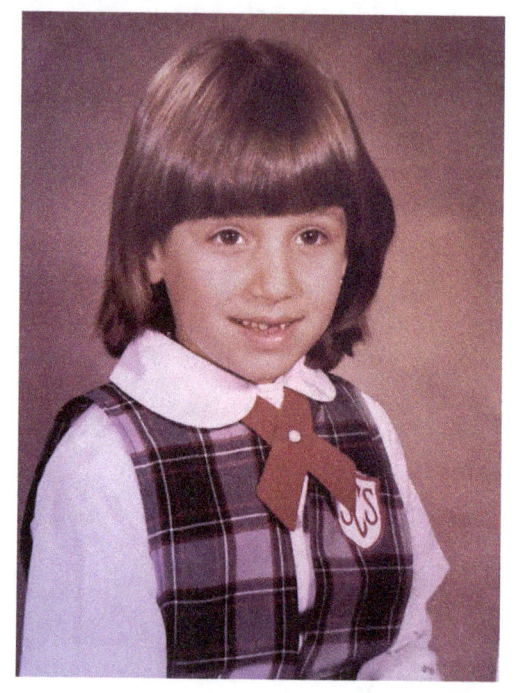

The author in elementary school

EXCERPT

In our neighborhood, there were several family members and friends from Italy, all within walking distance or a close drive. Everyone supported each other and made a little community in this small space of a town. Everyone helped each other and worked together to keep every tradition alive. [....] I was surrounded by my family and my culture, and assimilating to the American way of life was not really what we did. It was not quite that melting pot that people talk about; that took many more years to happen.

Il Dolce (The Sweet)

[Italian]

Milena Perna Scalzo

I was born at Mercy Hospital in Rockville Centre, New York; however, most of my childhood I felt out of place and like I was a foreigner in my own country. My parents came from a small town in Italy—Lioni, Avellino—and made their way over to America to have a better life that included work and prosperity. Many of our family members had come over to America before them, and so they were following in the footsteps of cousins, aunts, and uncles, who wrote about the opportunities that could be found here in this grand place called America.

I was born a few years after my parents and grandparents had settled on Taft Street in West Hempstead. In our neighborhood, there were several family members and friends from Italy, all within walking distance or a close drive. Everyone supported each other and made a little community in this small space of a town. Everyone helped each other and worked together to keep every tradition alive—making sauce, bottling wine—and we had our own little Italy in our neighborhood (small vineyards hanging over patios, tomato plants, and gardens filled with peppers and lettuces, La Befana, pasquetta, …). I was surrounded by my family and my culture, and assimilating to the American way of life was not really what we did. It was not quite that melting pot that people talk about; that took many more years to happen.

One of my most vivid memories of feeling so very different from other children was when I started kindergarten. I arrived speaking little to no English. Why did I need to speak English? For the last 5 years, everyone around me was Italian …. I had learned a little English but not much. My teacher, Sister Rosemary, I will never forget her, was not thrilled with my lack of language skills and my inability to understand how things worked in this "Country," not my country. It was time to color the letter D and write the letter D, and that came with a beautiful picture of a donut. It had to be colored precisely … inside the lines.

I recall Sister Rosemary was quite clear that neatness and precision were most important. Even speaking little English, I know what mattered to her. I needed to be like everyone else and step into line carefully. Well, on that day, I stared at the image on the page …. I had no idea what a donut was. I knew biscotti, I knew a cornetto … I ate cookies and milk with a dab of espresso for breakfast each morning. However, "donuts" with an odd shape did not make sense to me. I began to color neatly and colored the entire picture carefully, but I made one very big error on this specific day. I colored *the inside* of a donut. I did not know

SECTION 1: Challenges and Hardships

what a donut looked like, I had never been to Dunkin' Donuts before, and I had never eaten a donut in my life! So, Sister Rosemary proceeded to berate me and tell the class what NOT to do: "Please children, DO NOT color the inside of a donut, a donut has a hole. Leave the hole blank. DO NOT do what Milena has done." My heart sank, and that memory and that moment have lived with me to this day.

That day I left school wondering what other things I had never seen or heard of. I will never forget how alone and scared I felt because I was different and lived differently than my peers. That night, on my homework page, I made certain to color the donut carefully with the hole left blank and void of color. I told my mother about my day and how I had gotten into trouble. My mother shook her head and said, "Cosa? Ti ha messo nei guai a causa di un dolce?" She laughed and moved on quickly because this to her was so silly—a sweet had gotten her daughter into trouble! I can imagine how ridiculous this sounded to her.

The *Il Dolce* experience, though, has shaped me as a person and as an educator. I always knew from a young age that I wanted to become a teacher, that I wanted to spend my days with children. My goal was always to lift children up and show them all the gifts they had to give. It just so happens that I was offered my very first teaching job right as I completed my master's in education. I was asked to teach a kindergarten class, my absolute dream job! I was 22 years old and ready for this amazing opportunity. My very first teaching position, how ironic, was the exact grade that had impacted me in a powerful way; it was meant to be so. I started that year with that profound memory in mind. I made a choice to be a joyful, empathetic presence in the life of my students and I continue to do that every day. My promise to my students is always to understand, listen, and inspire them to love learning and themselves. It is my philosophy that in loving, understanding, and respecting our differences, we grow together and create the most amazing learning community.

Being a child of immigrants left me feeling like I was constantly trying to keep up, to figure out what I was missing. I was constantly trying to educate my parents so that I could fit in. Now, as an adult, I realize I was not missing anything. I was the lucky one blessed with culture, focused on family, and immersed in traditions that still live on in our family today. My parents gave me a true gift, a gift I cherish and continue to share with my own children.

Alfredo Vinci

Alfredo Vinci was born to Giuseppina and Arturo Vinci on April 5, 1973. His parents immigrated from different parts of Sicily—his mom from Alcamo in 1962 and his dad from Siracusa in 1968. They were married in St. Brigid's church in Bushwick, Brooklyn, which is where Alfredo ended up getting married 30 years later. Alfredo grew up in a traditional Italian family and started kindergarten speaking only Italian. Fortunately, the school had a bilingual Italian program. He ended up graduating Grover Cleveland HS. He currently lives on Long Island with his wife and three sons and has his own deli delivery route.

A picture of the author with his parents, Giuseppina and Arturo Vinci

EXCERPT

For every major event in our family, such as weddings, communions, confirmations, baptism, mom had a little notepad that she would keep in her dining room drawer. It included a list of family members, and how much each gave as a financial gift as well as how many people attended every event. Nonmonetary gifts were frowned upon. Thus, when they invited us to their parties and it was mom's turn to return the gifts, she would refer to her little notepad, and they would not get a penny more than what they gave us (per person).

Save, Save, Save

[Italian]

Alfredo Vinci

From the moment I was born I felt like I had to go to work and stretch the dollar as much as possible. This obsession my parents had with money proved to be a great thing and a not-so-great thing.

Let's go back to the beginning ….

My parents immigrated here from two different towns in Sicily, Italy. My mother, Giuseppina, came to the United States from Alcamo, at age 17 in 1962. My dad, Arturo, came from Siracusa at age 27 in 1968. Both spoke no English. Mom had a second-grade education. She could not read or write in English and barely in Italian. Dad had no education and could not read or write in Italian either. He ended up attending night school when coming to the United States and learned enough English (speaking, reading, and writing) to get by. Mom also learned enough English to get by just by working in a factory.

In July 1968, my parents met through a coworker from the factory she worked at. They got married in November 1968. As they had no savings, they paid the caterers using the money that they got from the wedding. My mother, my nonna and nonno, and my uncle Tony saved up to buy a six-family building in Ridgewood, Queens, which they shared. Through several different jobs that my dad had, and my mom's factory job, my parents had saved enough money to buy three more houses.

Mom never bought anything full price. She has a gift for haggling, even in places where you aren't allowed to haggle. If she didn't like the price, she would let the clerk know that she wasn't buying that item and let them know where she was going. "I'ma go across the street" she would say in her broken English. She was a seamstress by trade and was used to haggling on Delancey Street. We would ride the M train to Delancey, and she would give me a lesson on how she wasn't going to pay what they told her to pay. Still today … she haggles.

Mom worked in a suit factory, and she made 5 cents for every suit that she completed. Therefore, she wanted that 5 cents to be stretched as far as possible. She clipped coupons and went to several stores to compare prices. My father even has a joke, "se non ci fosse niente in vendita, moriremmo di fame" ("If nothing were on sale, we would starve"). My mother only buys things when they are on sale. Along the staircase in her basement, she would have ten bottles of laundry detergent. When I'd ask about it, she'd say, "What? It was on sale."

I grew up in Bushwick, Brooklyn. As I got older, I worked as many hours as I could. I got my first two jobs at age 12, one at a flower shop and the other at my uncle's pizzeria. My father always taught me, "any day you don't work is money lost." When I got paid, the money went directly to mom. She had a special account that she saved my money in. This, in turn, is a lesson I instilled in my children and thus created accounts for them when they were born.

We never ate out in restaurants. Why spend money when mom can make the same exact meal at home? My mother prides herself on her cooking. To this day, she does not eat in restaurants (except for a major event). "It's a waste of money," she says.

For every major event in our family, such as weddings, communions, confirmations, baptism, mom had a little notepad that she would keep in her dining room drawer. It included a list of family members, and how much each gave as a financial gift as well as how many people attended every event. Nonmonetary gifts were frowned upon. Thus, when they invited us to their parties and it was mom's turn to return the gifts, she would refer to her little notepad and they would not get a penny more than what they gave us (per person).

Now, let's fast-forward to my wanting to be the first in our immediate family to attend college. I took the SAT several times to get into the college I wanted. We got financial aid, so it wasn't expensive; but my parents were very upset that I chose college over work. Dad said, "Why are we paying money to school when you could be out working, making money." For them, who had no education, money was more important. Thus, I started working longer hours, plus attending school. I was exhausted, and school fell by the wayside. I went to work full time, not even finishing one year of college. This was a major mistake as I've been struggling ever since without a college degree and going from job to job.

I appreciate my parents' frugality, and how they taught me the value of a dollar. This I have instilled in my three children, and they each understand the value of a dollar as well. I see that in my two older boys, who, when they get paid from their jobs, do not want to spend any of their money and rather keep it in their bank account, only occasionally buying something for themselves.

However, unlike my parents, I encourage my boys to attend college or a trade school and get a good-paying job—call it a short-term loss for a long-term gain.

SECTION 1: Challenges and Hardships

Terry Stratoudakis

Terry Stratoudakis was born and raised in Queens, New York. His parents, Nick and Maria Stratoudakis, immigrated to the United States from Mournies, Chania in Crete, Greece in the 1970s. The wisdom of the ancient Greeks and folk traditions of Crete were part of his upbringing. Greek traditions and customs including food, dance, music, and history as well as speaking mostly Greek at home were part of growing up. Terry is a graduate of NYU Polytechnic University with an MS and BS in electrical engineering. He is a published author and has his own consulting company. He is most connected to his Greek heritage when cooking and sharing it with friends. Terry and his wife, Chrisa, live in Baltimore, Maryland.

The author with his parents, Maria and Nick Stratoudakis

EXCERPT

One day when I was a teenager, a salesperson called the house. Unfortunately for this caller, my mother picked up. I could not hear him, but I could tell from my mother's response that he was struggling with our last name. My mother unapologetically began to sound out the last name to him. Stra-too-da-kis, over and over. She then ordered him to use his phonics and then hung up on him. My mother and I had a really good laugh.

Alphabet

[Greek]

Terry Stratoudakis

"S, T like Tom, R, A, T like Tom, O, U, D like David, A, K, I, S." I don't know who said it first, my mother or my father. Always on the phone and most of the time in person, this was my introduction to my last name of Stratoudakis.

Back in the fifth grade, during gym class, I heard the teacher say the first name of a student and then say "alphabet." Then, as he reached me, he spoke my first name and then said "You too are an alphabet." I asked him why and he plainly said, "Your last name has all the letters in the alphabet." Initially, my 11-year-old mind took him too literally. Even with repetitions, I thought he was close enough. I felt a certain camaraderie with the other "alphabet" classmate who turned out to also be of Greek ancestry. Other teachers would always smile when they had to read my name during the taking of attendance. They knew we were Greek. In school and other places where I had to fill out my last name in forms, I was always the slowest because I was "writing out the alphabet."

Outside of school and then later in college, one could say that I'd heard it all. People reading my name did not want to spend time on it and would rush, so I would sometimes get "Stratoudowski" or other transformations. I was "Stratavarious" to the fans of classical music and "Stratocaster" to my rock 'n' roll friends. At a hotel, the receptionist said my name sounded like a dinosaur. My parents instilled a certain unassuming pride in my last name, so no matter how bad the butchering of my last name, it did not bother me. That extra time people spent on my last name meant they were trying. I do not think it is too difficult to say, especially if you sound it out, but I am biased. Certainly, if one is not used to longer last names, Stratoudakis could be a challenge. Whether people mispronounced it or not, I was always sympathetic. When asked my name, say, by a receptionist at the dentist's office, I simply hand over my driver's license.

One day when I was a teenager, a salesperson called the house. Unfortunately for this caller, my mother picked up. I could not hear him, but I could tell from my mother's response that he was struggling with our last name. My mother unapologetically began to sound out the last name to him. Stra-too-da-kis, over and over. She then ordered him to use his phonics and then hung up on him. My mother and I had a really good laugh.

The "-akis" suffix in my last name is characteristic of those from the island of Crete. Up to a certain age, I did not know the difference between Greece and Crete. A trip to Greece was really a trip to Crete and specifically the village of Mournies, just a few miles outside the city of Chania. If someone spoke Greek, I would tell my parents I met someone else from Crete.

Descending from Crete carries certain distinctions: home of the Minoan civilization, that of the original labyrinth and the resident Minotaur in Greek mythology, and that of ancient architects Daedalus and his son Icarus who flew too high. As an island in the middle of the Mediterranean Sea, Crete was occupied by various civilizations including that of Rome, Byzantium, Venice, and the Ottomans. Before joining Greece in the early 1900s, it even was its own republic.

Many famed Greeks hail from Crete, including Eleftherios Venizelos, prime minister of Greece during its expansion in the early 20th century and Nikos Kazantzakis, author of books such as *Zorba the Greek* and *The Last Temptation*. Crete is known for its hospitality. In the 20th century during World War II, the locals fought heroically alongside the Allied armed forces to defend the island in the eponymous Battle of Crete. The Venetians left many beautiful ports and architecture but also vendettas that have forced people to exile from their home island. In Crete, people fire guns on special occasions, such as weddings and christenings. Its natives express themselves with a 15-syllable *mantinada* (poem) for love, sorrow, and other human feelings. Foods such as *pilafi*, *tsigariasto*, and various pies are unique to the island. Traditional music, songs, dances, and costumes distinguish Crete from other parts of Greece. And yes, the names of many of the inhabitants of Crete have the suffix "-akis."

Learning about Crete always fascinated me. I enjoyed reading about the island but also talking about it with others. In one conversation, I came to know of a "little," no pun, dirty secret. The '-akis' suffix (little) has negative origins. It turns out that the Ottomans had bestowed this suffix on the Greeks of Crete to belittle them. This did not change how I saw myself or my last name. While I feel connected to Crete's history and heritage, the richness of the island was too much for the origin of my second name to put a damper on it for me. There is so much other history and heritage to be proud of. The Greek suffix -akis is much like the Spanish "ito," which also means little. Small is cute and concise, and right to the point. In Greece, one asks for a *petsetaki* (small napkin) or *kafedaki* (small coffee). The "-aki" suffix does not always signal smallness or refer to a belittling term.

In Crete, there are families without this suffix. Typically, these families were from the more remote and/or mountainous parts of the island. It is also likely that these families may have never been under the Ottoman rule. Never having been ruled by the Ottomans is certainly a source of pride for these families. I think of them as the highlanders of Crete.

During the 1980s, I remember going with my mother to pick up newly developed pictures and I was surprised to see that she used the last name Strat. Naturally, I inquired and found out that my parents had thought about officially shortening our last name to "Strat." I would not have been happy with this. Though they did not change it, I always wonder what my reaction would have been if they did. Would I have reverted mine? My full last name is a constant reminder of my heritage, and it connects me back to Greece and to my relatives with the same last name.

When I go back to Crete, to my parents' village, we are referred to as Stratoudis if there is just one of us or Stratoudides if more than one. I'd never know what I am, a Greek or an American, so I have settled with New Yorker, and though I no longer live in the city I was born in, it helps. I carry with me my Greek heritage and like to talk about it. I am cool about the various mispronunciations and transformations of my last name that I hear. With more things being set up online such as restaurant reservations, it is an exception rather than a rule that I need to sound out my last name. If it is in person, I just hand them my driver's license and let them copy it into their system.

Once when I was in Greece traveling without my parents, I was in a situation where I had to book my own hotel room. I arrived and the hotel receptionist asked for my last name. In Greek, I told him it is Stratoudakis. He immediately started to fill out the forms. He did not smile, look at me funnily, or ask me to spell it. I had never found spelling out my last name a chore, but at this moment, I took a break from spelling out the alphabet. A smile came over me, and I am not sure if the receptionist noticed it. I did not need to sound it out or spell it. It had never bothered me, but I did not hear any funny quotes or jokes about the Jurassic period. It was just another Greek name in Greece.

SECTION 1: Challenges and Hardships

Nazli Diba

Nazli Diba is the only child of Persian immigrants. Her family settled in the United States shortly after the Iranian Revolution of 1979. Her father, Mohsen Diba, an accountant for Iran Air, imbued his daughter with a love for travel. Growing up with two primarily Farsi-speaking parents in Queens, NY was a unique experience that led to a deep appreciation for not only the Persian culture but also the language and its delicious food. Nazli attributes a lot of her success to her family's strong support, both emotional and practical. Her father passed on these strong traditions by delivering homecooked Persian meals while Nazli was at college at Binghamton University, and studying for her master's degree at Buffalo University. The meals did not stop arriving while at Stony Brook University School of Dental Medicine or UCLA's AEGD residency. Her parents' tireless support continued on through her residency in pediatric dentistry. Nazli settled into living in Manhasset with her own family and practicing pediatric dentistry close to home. She now shares her love for her culture and its diverse experiences and flavors with her family and community.

The author with her father (baboo), Mohsen Diba

EXCERPT

My father reeked of garlic, always. It is very stereotypical for immigrants to smell like the flavors of their country. He would tell me the medicinal benefits of garlic—"It's penicillin, it boosts the immune system." Only years later could I appreciate this. That smell was one I never wanted to be around and now years after his passing, I crave for that smell.

Garlic

[Persian]

Nazli Diba

Garlic. That is one of the things that comes to mind when I think of my childhood. Garlic and foods that I shortly realized no other kids were eating, once I started school. The day I came home and saw cow brain in the fridge and was told it was "chicken cutlet" at dinner that night, I knew our family was different. My father reeked of garlic, always. It is very stereotypical for immigrants to smell like the flavors of their country. He would tell me the medicinal benefits of garlic—"It's penicillin, it boosts the immune system." Only years later could I appreciate this. That smell was one I never wanted to be around and now years after his passing, I crave for that smell.

My father, Mohsen Diba, was born in Tabriz, Iran on October 27, 1930. He was one of eight children—three sisters and five brothers. He was the oldest. I guess he was always used to being in charge because he was basically relied on to be leader among the children and had to help raise his siblings. He was responsible for keeping tabs on their whereabouts, making sure they went to school and behaved. He was also responsible for helping the family financially. My father was a very disciplined, commanding man. He went on to become an accountant. He worked for Iran Air at a time when travel was an event. He traveled back and forth to the United States often due to the then Shah's open regime. Iran Air's New York office was based in the Pan Am building, now the MetLife building on Park Ave. My father came to the United States as head accountant in charge of the NY office. Before the Revolution, my father flew freely between the United States and Iran. Once the Revolution occurred, he never went back. Since he was a supporter of the Shah, he was blacklisted and couldn't go back. The once free, Western, and modernized country that he loved turned into the controlling Islamic Republic. Until his dying day, he had hopes of seeing a free Iran, one that was like the one he grew up in.

My father met my mother, Fereshteh, who had left Iran when she was 16 years of age, in the 1970s. My mother came to the United States in hopes of a better life. Her brother had moved to California earlier and so my mom followed. She worked as a nanny for a nice family in Los Angeles. She worked on her English and earned her associate's degree.

I was born on August 23, 1974, in Brooklyn Hospital, New York. We lived in a two-bedroom apartment in Forest Hills, Queens. My life until kindergarten was typical, or so I thought. When I started school and realized everyone spoke English, I knew I was in trouble. My parents had only spoken to me in Farsi, so I had to take English as a Second

Language (ESL) classes upon entering the public school system. Navigating school was very hard for me. I was extremely envious of all the English-speaking kids at school—the kids who had help with their homework when they got home. I was on my own, and it was hard. My parents spoke English, but not to the point that was going to help me. As a matter of fact, as I got better and further in school, I had to help them. I was always embarrassed when I had to translate. My dad was always quick to go into argumentative mode when he missed what someone said or didn't understand something. I always had to defuse the situation. Thinking back, I wish I had done it with more pride.

There were other things that I was embarrassed about. My clothes were never the brand names other kids were wearing. My father was very economical. Clothes were considered functional and not for fashion. I was also made fun of for my name, a lot. I always wished my name had been one of the common ones. My mother told me that my father told the nurse "Nazli" as soon as she asked for a name. He had never even discussed it with her. He had it saved. It is of Turkish origin. Where my father grew up in Tabriz, they speak a form of Turkish, hence the name he had saved for me. No one at school could pronounce it. No one could spell it. It really bothered me growing up. At an age when anything that made you stand out was cause for bullying at school, it really wasn't a help to me. Years later, as I matured into adulthood, I realized what a gift my name really was.

In college, I realized that I did not want to be like everyone else. I wanted to stand out, and I grew to love my name. It was a topic that always sparked a conversation and led me to talk about my heritage. Every time someone heard my name, they wanted to know about my name and where I was from. Even though I was born here, I grew up with strong Persian values. I respected my parents and their expectations of me. I grew up listening to Persian music and celebrating our cultural holidays. I helped prepare Persian foods that always consisted of rice, stews, and various meats marinated in an array of Middle Eastern spices. All I wanted to do was fit in when I was younger, and now as an adult, I understand the gift I was handed by my parents. They instilled in me a strong sense of self and a strong foundation from which to grow. I love that I am now bilingual and can pass on the same values to my children.

I encourage my kids not to conform and to be proud of their Persian heritage. I keep cultural traditions alive and visit my children's classrooms to educate kids on Persian New Year. My youngest loves garlic and all things that pertain to Iran. My father reincarnated? I hope so ….

Polina Raya Oleynikova

Polina Raya Oleynikova, aged 16 years, is the daughter of Elena Oleynikova and Konstantin Oleynikova, who immigrated to the United States from Tashkent, Uzbekistan, after marriage, to start a family and give their children more opportunities than that they ever had. Residing in Queens, New York for most of her life, Polina grew up in a traditional Russian-speaking household. She loves her mom's cooking, as she prepares the best Uzbek dishes every day. Living in close proximity to her other family members and friends who either immigrated to the United States or are first generation, Polina loves spending time with her loved ones and bonding over shared experiences. Now residing in Long Island, Polina is a junior at North Shore High School in Long Island, NY. Living in a house in a quiet area is a drastic change from the urban streets Polina was used to. She loves her two cats, Lola and Leova, with all her heart and dreams of becoming a cat lady when she is older.

The author when she was little

EXCERPT

Looking back, my entire childhood was that of a child of immigrants, and I am not sure how blind I was to not recognize this until now. Having only Russian-speaking teachers for all extracurricular activities, eating only Uzbek cuisine at home, going to Hebrew Sunday school, and so on. It's pretty funny to look back on all of my memories as a kid and how they have shaped me into the person I am today.

Distant Memories

[Uzbek] [Student Essay]

Polina Oleynikova

Looking back, my entire childhood was that of a child of immigrants, and I am not sure how blind I was to not recognize this until now. Having only Russian-speaking teachers for all extracurricular activities, eating only Uzbek cuisine at home, going to Hebrew Sunday school, and so on. It's pretty funny to look back on all of my memories as a kid and how they have shaped me as the person I am today.

For instance, my very first words were "Кто там?" (Who's there?) as I learned the phrase my parents spoke numerous times when someone knocked on the front door of our two-bedroom apartment in Queens, New York … when I was 5 years old. Now, I know what you might be thinking: Something was wrong with that girl. However, to my parents' surprise, nothing was wrong; I simply chose not to speak. I would just stomp my foot every time I wanted something, and I would just whine all day. A perfect example of this super-embarrassing way of getting attention was the Hanukkah party my daycare hosted. My mom has it all documented on her old camera: All the children were dancing and singing to Russian folklore songs, but I would just run to my mom, grab onto her coat, whine, get pushed back to the group of kids by my mom, and then the cycle would just repeat itself over and over again.

My dad wasn't present as he was at one of his many jobs trying to contribute to our family of five. With no college degree, staying on a job proved to be quite a task for my dad. I'm not sure where I got this from, but by using the philosophy "bigger is better" (which in hindsight, I didn't even use correctly), I equated my dad having numerous jobs to him being the coolest person in the world. I bragged about him to all my classmates and teachers as they could only give me a sour expression in response. Me being me, I obviously thought that I left them speechless because they didn't know how to respond to my dad being so cool. A taxi driver, cop, banker, wedding host, comedian, waiter, GameStop owner, occasional news reporter, screenwriter, and I am most definitely missing a few more, but my dad was and still is my hero.

My mom, the classic strict immigrant parent, signed me up for all the extracurriculars including dance, gymnastics, math tutoring, karate, piano, and tennis. She cared about my grades, friends, school life, and so on. Being the eldest child, I was expected to do a mountain of chores every day before my mom came back home from work. While I was in middle school, I couldn't hang out with my friends much during the school week as I picked my sisters up from their school bus after school, fed them, made sure they did their homework, and so on. On top of all that, I was responsible for the dishes, vacuuming, mopping, and the overall task of making sure the house was nice and tidy (which it never was). When I was hanging out with my friends, I had to be home by sundown or else I would be in big trouble. I used to resent my mom for being the bad cop, but now I am so grateful because she really has transformed me into the person I am today. Disciplined and responsible, I am grateful for the attitude of orderly nature my parents programmed into my head when I was a young child. So many people I know who aren't first- or second-generation immigrants never had that in their lives and lack maturity and responsibility.

In elementary and middle school, the bonds I had with other Russian-speaking/Bukharan kids came naturally, even if their parents didn't immigrate from Uzbekistan like mine did. We laughed at the same jokes and had very similar experiences, the same household products, and same habits associated with each family member. I get so giddy thinking back as those times were the times I cherished my family the most. I was and still am so grateful to have such a beautiful culture and people with whom I can share my experiences. However, what made me especially value my culture were the experiences I had (or rather the lack of) when I moved to Long Island, New York at the age of 14.

Just starting high school was already a challenging task, but it was especially troublesome as the new kid. It was hard to fit in at first, as everyone's experiences at home were so different from mine and I kind of felt like an outsider. I still remember everyone's eyes on me as I casually spoke Russian on the phone to my mom on the lunch line. I felt immense fear as I didn't want to be different. I just wanted to fit in with everyone else. But I was never on the same playing field to begin with. No friends who shared similar experiences, no fellow Russian-speaking people, nothing of that sort.

At first, I felt ashamed of being a first-generation immigrant child, but due to the lack of diversity in my school and neighborhood, I started to feel sorry for the other kids who would never experience the joy I experienced through my very distinct experiences being from a family of immigrants. I started to look into my culture more, the specific regions my family were from, being proud of speaking another language at home. Being a first-generation immigrant child gave me immense pride, and the thing I am the proudest of is my family and the experiences they went through to be able to give my younger sisters and me the life that we live. I mean I am actually currently typing this essay out in my bedroom on the second floor of my beautiful house in Long Island!

Now a junior in high school, I found my community of friends in theater, and some of them are even second- and first-generation immigrants! My boyfriend, who goes to my school, is also a first-generation immigrant, as his parents are from Brazil, with Portuguese being his first language. It just goes to show that even in the dullest of places I can find the people that I could naturally bond with and be more appreciative of the diverse culture I come from. Memories last a lifetime, and I hope to make some beautiful ones this upcoming year.

Fond Childhood Memories of the Immigrant Community

Authentic Trilingual NYC Upbringing and Immersion into Sicilian Roots 29
    [Italian; Mexican]
    Silvia Rosselli Davi

Treasure Island, the Bronx 33
    [Mixed-European]
    Jean Ende

My Birthday 38
    [Greek]
    Vicky Giouroukakis

Bajan Memories: Always in My Heart 42
    [Bajan: Barbadian]
    Joy Scantlebury

Summers in Greece 48
    [Greek]
    Nadia Giannopoulos

Silvia Rosselli Davi

Silvia Davi is a global corporate communications, marketing, and business development professional with over 20 years of experience. She is a seasoned C-suite executive, entrepreneur, contributor, and board member, with a background that stems from leadership roles at top global communications consultancies, Fortune 500 organizations, start-ups, and nonprofits. As a multidimensional professional, Silvia has expertise in strategic public relations, branding, content, investor relations, capital markets, innovation, financial services, technology, and lifestyle, and has received numerous industry accolades for her work and achievements. Silvia resides in Manhasset, NY with her family.

The author with her children, Matteo and Silvana, in Sicily in front of the town's church doors crafted by her Nonno Carmelo Rosselli

EXCERPT

Astoria is a diverse neighborhood with groups of nationalities that assimilated over time. Today it may look like a melting pot, but the community I was raised in, mainly in the 1980s, was known for its early roots of working immigrants from Germany, Ireland, Italy, and Greece.

Authentic Trilingual NYC Upbringing and Immersion into Sicilian Roots

[Italian; Mexican]

Silvia Rosselli Davi

Growing up in Astoria, Queens was a distinctive NYC experience. I am the daughter of an Italian immigrant from Sicily and a teacher from Mexico City, who provided me with a beautiful, culturally rich upbringing. My family lived in an Italian American neighborhood surrounded by my paternal grandmother, cousins, aunts, uncles, and many *paesani* in a tightly knit community. In Queens, your neighborhood helps define your identity, and despite being a NY-born, Queens, Italian/Mexican girl, I belonged to an Italian, mainly Sicilian, area (Belluck, 1995). I was fascinated by the community fostered by Italian immigrants in the area, who cultivated an authentic cultural society passed on by immigrants and first- and second-generation Italian Americans.

Astoria is a diverse neighborhood with groups of nationalities that assimilated over time. Today it may look like a melting pot, but the community I was raised in, mainly in the 1980s, was known for its early roots of working immigrants from Germany, Ireland, Italy, and Greece. I grew up in a three-family house, purchased by my grandparents shortly after they immigrated to America from Castrofilippo, Sicily for a better life. My grandfather, *Nonno* Carmelo Rosselli, was an artisan and skilled carpenter, who secured a job in a Manhattan high-rise, and settled in Astoria, where many of his family members had migrated to over the years. Our community had a large population from my father's village of Castrofilippo, which included a social club to preserve customs. Even long-standing traditions such as an annual feast to honor the Sicilian town's patron saint, San Antonio Abate, were celebrated every June. The street fair was a high point during my childhood, and today, it's still held annually in Astoria's Ditmars area.

My immersive ethnic experience was unique, as my father had broken the mold and married outside of the Sicilian community, finding the love of his life while on vacation in Mexico. Unlike members in the neighborhood who would often go back to Italy to their native villages to find their match, my grandmother, *Nonna* Angela Rosselli, would explain how friends from Castrofilippo would inquire about my father, an eligible bachelor, as it was common for marriages to be arranged. My father resisted and chose to wait for his perfect pair, something my *Nonna* Angela understood quite well, as she herself resisted an arrangement and married her love, Carmelo. My grandfather (*Nonno*) passed the year I was born, and although I never met him, I was given Carmen as a middle name to honor him and was forever referred to as *Silvia di Carmine* by my *Nonna* Angela.

Growing up with my paternal grandmother, who lived in the apartment underneath ours, was delightful. My parents raised us in a compelling home, which somewhat differed from that of other immigrant families. In fact, I never considered my mother an immigrant. She would have never left her native Mexico City had she not fallen in love with a charming Italian tourist, my father, who was on the trip of his life to cheer on the Italian soccer team at the 1970 World Cup. My parents eventually married in Mexico City, then settled in Astoria, and it was a match made in heaven. I was their middle child in our family of five. While my father worked construction paving the streets of NYC, my mother ran our trilingual household like one of her classrooms, strict yet filled with activities. I spoke Spanish with my mom, Italian with my dad, and English with my siblings. My father, an intelligent and worldly man, ensured we learned history and factoids from both cultures. My parents sent us to Italian and Spanish schools once a week so that we could learn the foreign languages properly. Members of our community mainly spoke the Sicilian dialect; however, my parents insisted we speak in the proper languages, which was incredibly rewarding and today allows me to feel at home in multiple countries. Growing up, I was intrigued by the Sicilian dialect and made a concerted effort to learn it from my *Nonna* Angela. She only spoke in Sicilian, and I loved spending time with her. She was extremely animated, independent, and strong, and despite being half paralyzed, she was an active person and a phenomenal storyteller, attributes inherited also by my father. I would help *Nonna* make pizza, salt the eggplants, eat pastina, or just chat and snack on cheese, bread, and ripe tomatoes from her garden. Her *giardino* was a testament to the Castrofilippo countryside, with grapevines, peach, cherry, blackberry, and apple trees all planted by my *Nonno*. It was the perfect playground.

As a child in Astoria, I would regularly accompany my father to Broadway Street to purchase the Italian-American newspaper *Il Progresso* and fresh semolina bread from Parisi Bakery, where I was always greeted with a free Italian cookie, a highlight for me. Then we would cross the street to Dominick's Barbershop, to catch up with my father's Italian barbershop friends to discuss soccer and current events. He called me his *bambolina*—Italian for little doll. I was the only girl in the barbershop but loved every minute of it. The barbershop friends watched me grow up and celebrated my milestones. For instance, when I was featured in the *New York Daily News* in 1996 for my academic achievements and aspirations, my father was greatly celebrated. After moving to the Whitestone area in the 1990s, my dad would go back to the barbershop for family updates and, of course, to discuss soccer.

Despite the lack of Mexicans within my Queens community, my parents ensured we received a dose of our Mexican culture growing up by traveling annually to visit my grandparents and immerse in our other half. While, at times, Astoria felt like living in a small town in Sicily, it was only one bite of my "Big Apple" experience, given the proximity to Manhattan, my multilingual upbringing, and travels outside the country.

It's not surprising I married a first-generation Italian American, whose parents are also from Sicily from another small town called Borgetto. Vito and I purchased our first home in Whitestone, Queens, a newer Italian American hub with many Astoria transplants, and later moved to raise our children, Silvana and Matteo, to the suburb of Manhasset on Long Island's gold coast. Today, we take pride in how our kids love their culture(s), regularly visiting their two sets of grandparents in Queens. They look forward to stories told by their two Sicilian grandfathers, to authentic Mexican dishes by my mother, to the sacred Italian Sunday dinners cooked by their *Nonna* Sarina. But, most of all, they love their annual tradition of making and jarring fresh tomato sauce with the extended family (and, yes, it's sauce not gravy). Today, I'm proud to say that my daughter graduated Manhasset High School as president of the Italian Honor Society and is currently an Italian tutor at her university, while my son is an A+ Italian student at his middle school.

For more than two decades, my husband and I have traveled globally, covering most of Italy. This past summer, our two children urged us to return to Sicily to revisit their origins. A highlight of our vacation was witnessing their enthusiasm visiting both Castrofilippo and Borgetto, the two tiny villages where their three grandparents were born. On a more personal note, I will forever treasure taking them to the San Antonio Abate church in Castrofilippo to see the hand-carved doors made by my *Nonno* Carmelo Rosselli, the talented skilled carpenter who brought his family to New York. It was an extraordinary and full-circle moment, which I will cherish for the rest of my life.

References

Belluck, P. (1995). Distant but loyal: Little Sicily in Queens; Immigrants congregate but leave their hearts in Castrofilippo. *The New York Times*. www.nytimes.com/1995/07/17/nyregion/distant-but-loyal-little-sicily-queens-immigrants-congregate-astoria-but-leave.html

Jean Ende

Jean Ende is a native New Yorker who is trying to exercise her background by writing about her immigrant Jewish family. She's a former newspaper reporter, political publicist, corporate marketing executive, and college professor. Now retired and concentrating on her writing, she has published more than a dozen stories in print and online magazines, anthologies and has been recognized in literary competitions. She recently completed a family saga and is looking for an agent and/or publisher. Jean and her dog (which she eventually obtained despite her mother's objections) now live in Brooklyn, which is a foreign country to anyone from the Bronx.

The author with her dog

EXCERPT

I read about moms who could play tennis, adventures in college dorms, and a world where athletics were as important as academics. The people in the books on aunt Gussie's shelves had native English-speaking grandparents—a species I'd never encountered. The people in my neighborhood were Jewish or Italian. We all had stout, corseted mothers who believed in the benefit of large portions of high-carb foods and extra sweaters to protect us from unmentionable diseases. We had distant fathers who worked hard and therefore deserved respect, and grandparents who spoke English with heavy accents and frequently switched to another language mid-sentence. My family had come to this country dreaming of an America where the streets were paved with gold. Their heavily accented voices echoed in my head while I read and had visions of the "real" America.

Treasure Island, The Bronx

[Mixed European]

Jean Ende

If a Jewish pirate decided to retire to the Bronx, he and his wife, who was also a pirate, would probably be a lot like my Great Aunt Gussie and Uncle Harry. Aunt Gussie had a black plastic patch over one lens of her glasses, Uncle Harry walked with a limp.

Their house was the perfect place to store treasure, a tall castle in a deserted area where few people went because it was protected by thick, thorny bushes and a screechy copper-colored dragon.

Well, anyway that's what I believed when I was 10, 11, and 12 years old and spent much too much time daydreaming for someone my age, according to my mother.

Today, I know that Aunt Gussie wore a patch because she hadn't received proper treatment for an eye infection when she was young and she got dizzy if she used the weak eye, and Uncle Harry walked with a limp because he had arthritis in his left knee.

Today, I know that the house they lived in is called a Tudor and was located at the border of the North Bronx and Westchester County and few people went there because there wasn't much there. I know that the thorny bushes in their yard were where the currants grew that Aunt Gussie used to make jelly, and that the dragon's head doorknocker screeched because Uncle Harry forgot to oil it.

Great Uncle Harry was my Grandma Leah's older brother, and he was as skinny as she was fat. He wore bowties and pants that were too big for him. Harry and my Grandma Leah had come to America from Poland when Grandma was 16 years old and he was 20 years old, just the two of them. Harry was supposed to work hard and start a business for the rest of the family to work in and Grandma would help him. The rest of their family remained in Warsaw while their father settled his affairs. But he waited too long. Grandma and Uncle Harry's parents, their other brothers and sisters, were all lost in the war.

Many of my relatives were lost in the war. When I was young, I imagined a crowd of confused old people wandering around Europe, knocking on doors, and peering around corners while guns fired and planes dropped bombs; going from village to village in Poland and Hungary, and Russia and Romania, trying to find their way home.

Grandma told me that when she and Harry made the trip to America she was often scared of the big ocean and the way the boat sometimes rocked, so he held her hand and sang to her to keep her calm. I stared at Uncle Harry's hands that were stiff and bent into clawlike shapes. I couldn't imagine anyone wanting to hold those hands. I never heard Uncle Harry sing.

SECTION 2: Fond Childhood Memories of the Immigrant Community

Aunt Gussie's family had come to New York from Germany, which, I'd been told meant that they thought they were high class, at least higher than my father's family which had come from a small village in Poland. Aunt Gussie had gone to university in Germany and there were people in her family who were professors, ballerinas, and opera singers. We didn't see those people very often.

When Aunt Gussie's family decided it wasn't safe to be a Jew in Germany, they contacted relatives who were already in the United States and could help them get settled. But they were never again as rich as they had been in Germany.

Harry and Gussie's home was furnished with thick oriental rugs, and their cabinets held fine China and crystal glasses. But as I got older, I noticed that the rugs were worn, the rooms needed painting, and the sets of China and silverware were incomplete.

Grandma Leah told me that Aunt Gussie's family wasn't happy when she started going out with Harry, a boy from Poland whom she had met at the local library. They agreed to the marriage because Harry had a successful business and, even though she was educated and came from a good family, Gussie was a girl with a bad eye who might not be able to attract one of the wealthy *Deutsche Yidden*, German Jewish men.

Grandma and I made the trip to their house every other month. Just the two of us. Grandpa Jake was dead, and my parents were too busy to go. As far as I was concerned, this was the perfect arrangement. Gussie and Harry's house really was filled with treasures that I had no desire to share with anyone.

When we got off the train, I'd lead my grandma to the hill on top of which was Aunt Gussie and Uncle Harry's house and reach up to the doorknocker, lift the dragon's big head, and listen to him screech.

Aunt Gussie smelled better than other old ladies. Instead of chicken fat and parsley, she smelled of the fine, white, lilac-scented powder that came from a silver box with a large powder puff. The box was in her bedroom, on her dresser, on a blue-mirrored tray. I'd never seen a blue mirror before, it made me look like someone in a fairy tale. I was allowed to use the powder, since Aunt Gussie knew I'd be careful and wouldn't spill any. If I did spill, I blew the powder away before anyone noticed.

When Grandma and Uncle Harry and Aunt Gussie talked to each other they spoke in English. My mother had explained to me that Jewish people from Germany didn't speak Yiddish; they considered it a lower-class language. Unless there was someone in the room who wasn't Jewish, all the other old people I knew spoke to each other only in Yiddish.

While the grown-ups had tea and talked about whatever it was that grown-ups talk about, I could go into the garden, pretend I was a soldier and battle my way through the thorny bushes that guarded tiny black and red berries that shown like jewels. I learned to pry apart the tangled branches carefully, so my hands didn't get scratched. No one noticed if I picked these berries; no one noticed if I ate them without washing them first.

When I was tired of being outside, I went to the living room where there was an old, upright piano painted light green with tiny pink roses. If you didn't know any better, you might think that the color was the only thing special about this piano and you'd press the keys and make ordinary piano sounds. But Aunt Gussie had shown me that the piano had a magic switch. When you pressed the switch and pumped the pedals, the keys went up and down and the piano played songs all by itself. I tried to memorize the keys' motions, so the next time we visited, I could get my fingers on to the right keys and look like I was really playing.

The best part of the house was the top floor. Up two flights of worn wooden steps was a big room with a whole wall of bookcases that reached almost to the ceiling, just like the ones in the public library.

In my house we had an encyclopedia, schoolbooks, and some paperback books my mother bought at the drug store. On the shelves in Harry and Gussie's house were stacks of yellowing magazines, books with old leather bindings, shiny, new, hardcover books, and lots of thick paperbacks.

There was a large collection of *Reader's Digest Condensed Books*. I never thought about what "condensed" meant, that there might be something missing from these stories; I was too impressed by the idea of so many stories, three or four in each plastic-covered volume. There were all kinds of books and no one to tell me to do my homework, or clean my room, or do anything but open a book and ignore everything else.

In Aunt Gussie's library, there were books about Eskimos and Indians, stories that took place in Europe, Asia, and Africa, and sci-fi books about outer space. But these were of minor interest. I became a connoisseur of novels that took place in even more exotic locales—like the Midwest—and featured strange people with strange folkways. I later learned they were called WASPs. I searched for stories that took place in Iowa, or Kansas, or Utah, all the square states I'd mix up in find-the-states jigsaw puzzles.

I read about moms who could play tennis, adventures in college dorms, and a world where athletics were as important as academics. The people in the books on Aunt Gussie's shelves had native English-speaking grandparents—a species I'd never encountered.

The people in my neighborhood were Jewish or Italian. We all had stout, corseted mothers who believed in the benefit of large portions of high carb foods and extra sweaters to protect us from unmentionable diseases. We had distant fathers who worked hard and therefore deserved respect, and grandparents who spoke English with heavy accents and frequently switched to another language mid-sentence.

My family had come to this country dreaming of an America where the streets were paved with gold. Their heavily accented voices echoed in my head while I read and had visions of the "real" America.

I wanted to live among people with perfect enunciation, people with short, easy-to-pronounce names and to be one of the slim, blonde girls *(If you don't eat, people will think you have consumption)*.

I pictured myself throwing a stick retrieved by a dog named Prince ("A dog, what do you want with a dog? It'll poop on the carpet, shed on the couch, and set off your allergies").

I longed for camping trips ("Sleep outside where animals can eat you? I warn you about rashes you can get from strange toilet seats, and you want to pee in the woods?").

I tried to learn high jumps so that I could become a cheerleader for the high school football team ("A bunch of goyim chasing a lopsided ball and jumping all over each other. With what they're doing to their hands you think they'll become surgeons?").

Just once, instead of being urged to have a third helping of overcooked meat and vegetables, I wanted to sit down to a meal of a cheeseburger and fries and a tall glass of milk ("***###!! Where do you get such an idea?").

I sat in the creaky old rocking chair reading those books until it was time to go home. Sometimes, I asked Aunt Gussie if I could borrow a book, and she always said yes.

And that night I dreamed of being a pirate who sailed on the amber waves of grain where loaves of white bread grew.

Editor's Essay

EXCERPT

We enter our home, the smallest apartment, a railroad apartment, as I discover years later, but to me, it doesn't matter. Hurrying to the kitchen because there are so many groceries to unpack. Mom quickly organizes the ingredients for our meal, preparing the menu—spanakopita, tiropita, loukaniko, pastitsio, aaaaand cake, of course!

My cake and five candles.

It's my birthday! I can't wait for my party!

The author as a little girl

My Birthday

[Greek]

Vicky Giouroukakis

Ditmars and 31st Street, Astoria, NY. This is where I was born and raised until I was 8 years old. The best of times and the worst of times. One of several apartment buildings in a row that, a few years later, became subsidized housing for the poor.

Fifth floor, 5D, no elevator. Saturday, January 8. Mom carries groceries up the steep steps, two young kids in tow. First floor, second floor, third floor, fourth floor, fifth floor.

Phew!

We made it!

Sweat and palpitating heart!

Wait, we have a visitor outside our door again.

The bearded homeless man dressed in a hunter-green tracksuit is sleeping on his side on the staircase, stinking of pee. Mom, breathing heavily now, puts the groceries down, searches for the keys in her bag, takes them out, and fumbles to open the door.

Quietly.

Steadily.

"Shh …. Don't wake up the homeless man because you don't know what he might do. A stranger, after all."

Dangerous?

Who knows?

In this neighborhood, anything is possible.

Mom opens the door hurriedly, maniacally. She pulls us into the apartment and then the groceries. The door locks shut.

Boom.

Homeless man out of our sight and out of our minds.

We enter our home, the smallest apartment, a railroad apartment, as I discover years later, but to me, it doesn't matter. Hurrying to the kitchen because there are so many groceries to unpack. Mom quickly organizes the ingredients for our meal, preparing the menu—spanakopita, *tiropita*, *loukaniko*, pastitsio, aaaaand cake, of course!

My cake and five candles.

It's my birthday! I can't wait for my party!

My brother, Steve, tries on one of the birthday hats for my friends, looks in the mirror, smirks, rolls his eyes, and then takes it off. Too babyish for his 10-year-old self.

Too little time but so much to do. Clean the apartment, cook, set the table, blow up the balloons, and decorate.

After three hours of prepping, we open the door. No sign of the homeless man. Maybe he is hiding, or maybe he gets scared by all the noise and leaves. The guests start arriving, shuttling in one by one.

First, my favorite cousin Stacy and her sister, Demetra, from upper, well-to-do Ditmars with their silky brown bobs and their identical baby blue coats with fur trim, and their mom wearing a long-belted camel hair coat that matches her tan complexion. Too pretty and fine in contrast to the drab furniture and my lacy, ornate dress that screams, *you are trying too hard.*

Then, my best friend, Stamatoula, who lives in 4C, comes with her pink petticoat to show it off as if she comes from outside and not the floor below. An only child, she has all the best toys and clothes I can never imagine owning.

Stamatoula has a hard time sharing, and one day I go to play with her Play-Doh oven playset, and she yells at me for touching it! I get up, tears rolling down my face, and leave quietly. On the way out, as soon as I get to the door, her mom asks in a sweet voice, "Are you OK?" "I am fine," I say in a low voice, hiding my tears and my hurt.

I knew then the boundaries that defined our friendship.

Oh, and Mrs. Belize from 5C arrives with her white powdery face, bright red lips, short black hair pulled back, and wearing a white nightrobe buttoned down in the middle. The one who would help us with our homework when we need her because our parents can't. When she comes near, the combined smell of cigarettes, strong floral perfume, and red chalky lipstick makes me dizzy.

My father eventually sneaks inside, hurries to his bedroom to change out of his pizzaman uniform and clean up, and then appears relaxed, smooth, as if he is always in the apartment and not at his 12-hour shift standing the whole time in front of a hot stove making and serving pizza.

Kalosirthate, kalosirthate (Welcome, welcome), he says in Greek. How are you? Good? Broad smile on his face that never fades. Oh, Dad! Always putting on the widest smile when he sees a dear friend or relative or meets someone new for the first time. His chest expands as if his heart is opening wide to receive love like a seashell opening up for nourishment.

All the guests finally arrive, and there is chatter and noise. Stamatoula, Stacy, Demetra, Eleni, and I play ring-around-the-rosy in one of the living room corners. A couple of toddlers in the mix wail, cry, and then laugh. Steve and his friend, Demetri, chase each other with darts, crashing into everyone.

"Hey, stop that!" someone shouts.

Adults drink wine and talk loudly, waving their hands, as most Greeks do, making wowing sounds while tasting mom's food. "Dina, the best cook!" they exclaim. Mom smiles proudly and brings out more food, forcing everyone to eat and eat, occasionally spoon-feeding people.

"I made the rice pudding with orange rind and juice," she say.

What great satisfaction it gives her, feeding people—as if this is her true mission in life, to satiate the world with her remarkable cooking. Then, the Greek music playing in the background inspires someone, usually my father, to start dancing, and then two, three, or four people move to the rhythm of the drunken sailor dance, which is an improvised dance with no prescribed steps. Like an eagle, arms out, back slightly bent, eyes looking down, and then steps forward, back, side, then twirl.

"Opa, Opa!" Then the traditional slap on the foot.

And me, sitting in the middle of the living room couch, taking in the melodious-to-my-ears sounds, grinning, watching my guests be merry, waiting for the frosted vanilla cake to come out so that they can sing "Happy Birthday." How many people are squeezed into this tiny space?

Dear God.

But nobody seems to mind the cramped arrangements. They have come here for me.

Happy birthday, dear Vicky. Happy birthday to you!

Joy Scantlebury

Joy Scantlebury is the daughter of the late Rev. Canon Cecil Alvin and Elizabeth Scantlebury, who emigrated to the United States from Barbados. Joy and her sister, Monica, learned the importance of education, diligence, family connection, and spirituality. Yearly summer trips to Barbados provided valuable connections with grandparents, aunts, uncles, and cousins. Joy is an English as a New Language (ENL) teacher at Pocantico Hills School in Westchester, NY. Her interest to write was inspired by listening to her parents' vivid stories about their formative years in Barbados. Joy has a strong appreciation for different cultures and the power of storytelling. She has an MA in TESOL from Teachers College, Columbia University and an MS in education from SUNY New Paltz.

The author with her parents, Rev. Canon Cecil Alvin and Elizabeth Scantlebury, and her sister Monica (behind the author)

EXCERPT

Storytelling is a Bajan art form. I never tire of hearing my mother's stories. Cooking evokes childhood stories. Even though my sister and I were born in the United States, we could imagine ourselves gazing at the crystal blue waters just like she did. As a child growing up on the island of Barbados, my mother enjoyed retreating to this inner world in which she imagined all sorts of things. "America offered more opportunities. I wanted to see what I could be."

Bajan Memories: Always in My Heart

[Bajan: Barbadian]

Joy Scantlebury

Clink. Clink. Clink. My mother's gold bangles jingle on her wrist as she turns off the Kitchen Aid mixer, lifts the nozzle, and stirs the batter. As she pours, it ripples down into the baking pan. "This cake will be done in two shakes," she says as she bangs the pan on the counter to smooth out the lumps. I put down the plantain I have been cutting and walk over to her makeshift workstation to observe her handiwork. A gust of warm air shoots out as she opens the oven door and slides the cake pan in. She sets her white Lux Minute Minder timer for 60 minutes. While the timer starts ticking, she whisks around to raise the heat on the pigeon peas and stir the sorrel simmering on the stove. Other Bajan delicacies are cooling on the counter: cassava pone and "black cake" (or fruit cake).

It is Christmas Day. I still feel giddy from opening the Christmas presents several hours ago. My incessant pestering for a Holly Hobbie doll resulted in my very own doll awaiting me under the Christmas tree. Little did I know that my mother had been secretly making the doll by hand for several months. Every detail from the button eyes to the pinafore were meticulously hand-stitched and sewn on her Singer sewing machine.

Now I am in the kitchen "helping" my mother. At nine years old, I am not able to handle the intricacies of Bajan cuisine. My skills, however, are useful for simple tasks such as slicing plantain under her watchful eye.

Bustling in the kitchen since 8:00 a.m., my mother has already baked the turkey and ham as well as a pot full of peas and rice. She has also made the batter for the cod fish cakes. My mother is a dynamo to behold as she multitasks with ease. I am amazed by her indefatigable spirit. The previous day she made a variety of desserts to serve to parishioners after the Christmas Eve service at the Episcopal church where my father is the rector. The intermingling aromas of citrus and coconut swirl around the kitchen. It smells heavenly.

I return to sitting on a small stool next to a corner table and resume cutting the plantain. As if my mother has an internal timer, she swoops in to check my work. "You should cut the plantain at an angle," she suggests as I struggle. I have made disks instead of the oval slices she prefers. She grabs the plantain out of my hand. I watch as she deftly demonstrates how to cut it at an angle as the bangles go clink, clink, clink. She hands the plantain and knife to me as I clumsily clutch them. I attempt to slice the plantain at an angle, but somehow the jagged pieces pale in comparison. "You shouldn't cut it so thick, or else it won't fry correctly." It becomes clear that I have not inherited my mother's natural culinary skills, but what I have inherited is her determination. My brow furrows as I slice a few more pieces.

This time the slices look slightly better. "OK. Keep cutting while I check on the pigeon peas." She takes a spoon and pokes the green pigeon peas, which are furiously boiling on the stove. She sees that they are cooked and ready to make "jug jug." She bought a new attachment for grinding peas and meat on her Sunbeam Mixmaster, which will result in a thick consistency known as "jug jug." It is a deliberate process. The Bajan seasoning and guinea corn patiently sit on the counter awaiting their turn in the grinder.

In the dining room sitting on a mahogany chair, which my father made by hand, my 15-year-old sister, Monica, is grating coconut for the coconut bread, or "sweet bread." It is a monotonous task, but the upbeat calypso sounds playing on the record player create a festive atmosphere.

We are spending this Christmas in White Plains, New York. We will not go "home" to Barbados as we had the previous year. At that time, my mother had insisted that we fly on British West Indies Airways, or BWIA. Even though there was a joke among West Indians that "Bee Wee" flights were often delayed, my mother was adamant about giving them her business. Upon stepping onboard the plane, I soon understood her reasoning. We were met with beautiful, brown-skinned flight attendants impeccably dressed in multicolored uniforms who greeted us in mellifluous singsong. I had never seen flight attendants of color before. When they found out that it was our first time flying on the airline, they took a photo with Monica and me. When we landed, our family was there to greet us. That was the beginning of a flurry of visits with our grandparents, aunts, uncles, and cousins accompanied by a culinary array with Christmas melodies playing on the radio. Listening to "White Christmas" while beholding the "snow on the mountain" plant, which was in full bloom, was surreal. The spirit of Barbados infused the atmosphere through the voices of the Merrymen singing, "I gon' wake up early, bake me jug and me turkey. It's Christmas in my Caribbean land."

Back in White Plains, I hear the faint squeak of rattan cane being woven on chair seats coming from the basement. My father must be creating another chair. His father was a joiner in Barbados, who often enlisted his sons to learn the art of furniture making. My father always reminded me that furniture making required discipline. In essence, he was continuing his father's legacy. My father's workmanship is exhibited throughout our house. His masterpieces include the sofa, coffee table, and several rocking chairs. My father also has a penchant for salvaging discarded furniture from the roadside and fully refurbishing them. I marveled at how he juggled being a full-time rector with his furniture-making business. Late at night, I would hear him working on a chair, or the plink of the piano keys as he composed another hymn. He also built his own pulpit from which he preached his sermons. "Your father is a jack of all trades," my mom would say.

Now that my task is done, I watch as my mother drains the peas from the boiling water to prepare them for the grinder. "When did you know you wanted to come to America?" I ask. She replies, "Since I was a teenager. I would look out at the ocean and wonder what lay beyond the horizon." This is a story with which I am already familiar. Storytelling is a Bajan art form.

I never tire of hearing my mother's stories. Cooking evokes childhood stories. Even though my sister and I were born in the United States, we could imagine ourselves gazing at the crystal blue waters just like she did. As a child growing up on the island of Barbados, my mother enjoyed retreating to this inner world in which she imagined all sorts of things. "America offered more opportunities. I wanted to see what I could be." She would eventually become a registered nurse who worked in a school. When she envisioned a goal, she would make every effort to achieve it. Her determination to go to America was no different.

"Then I met your father."

"How did that happen?" This was a part of the story I did not know."

"He was a student at Codrington, and …."

" … and you saw him, looking handsome wearing his green shirt!" I blurt out. Codrington College was the oldest Anglican theological college in the Western Hemisphere, located in my mother's home parish of St. John.

"How did you know he wore a green shirt? I never told you that before."

It is true. I have no idea why I envision my father wearing a green shirt. I think it is because he likes the color green.

"Your father visited our home sometimes. Then my paperwork was processed, and I went to New York to live with uncle Henry and aunt May. Your father and I corresponded …."

Despite having seen him a few times, my mother knew there was something special about my father. She always told her mother that she wanted to marry a gentleman. Coincidentally, my mother's father was also a joiner. After completing seminary and becoming ordained, my father was assigned to a position at a church in Guyana. By the time my mother returned to Barbados on a visit several years later, she reunited with him, and they were soon engaged and then married at St. Martin's Church in Harlem.

As if on cue, I hear the tap, tap of my father's soft footsteps ascending the basement stairs as the Merrymen's up-tempo calypso, "Happy Birthday Jesus" starts playing. The sleeves of his black and red plaid flannel shirt are rolled up and specks of wood are visible on his sleeves.

"I'm going to go and change my clothes," he states.

The syncopated rhythm is infectious. When there is a calypso playing, my mom cannot resist.

"Let's dance!" she exclaims as she grabs my father's arm.

"Oh shucks," my father laughs as they whisk around the kitchen.

Monica and I exchange glances and giggle.

At 5:00 p.m., my father lights the firewood in the living room fireplace. He is wearing his clerical attire. We do not have chestnuts roasting, but it seems fitting to play Nat King Cole's Christmas album on the record player. As the fireplace crackles, I place the needle on the record. The violin strings play the opening measures of "The Christmas Song." As Nat sings, "Chestnuts roasting on an open fire," my father asks: "Do you notice Nat's enunciation?" Adding for emphasis, "His singing is perfection. You can understand every word he sings!"

I nod my head in agreement because I know he is correct in his analysis of Nat's brilliance. Nat's singing is quite the opposite of some of my favorite pop stars, whose "mumbling" and "screeching" make my father cringe. "You call THAT singing?" he would say.

Years later, I truly appreciate Nat King Cole's captivating voice and virtuosity, thanks to my father's music lectures. Sometimes, we would listen to classical station, WQXR, and play "name that composer." As someone who studied Greek, Latin, German, Hebrew, and French at Codrington College, my father had a great appreciation of language. No wonder he wrote so well, as evidenced in his published letters to the editor of the local paper and his eloquent, erudite sermons.

Sizzling and spirited chatter float from the kitchen. When I poke my head in, I see my mother donning one of her handmade red caftans and hair swept up into a bun. She is frying the codfish cakes while talking on the phone with one of her brothers who lives in Barbados. This is the fifth phone call from our family members in Barbados. As she sucks her teeth in a chupse, "Wuh law! Wuh law! Fuh true?" she responds as my uncle updates her on friends in the neighborhood where she grew up.

Monica places a red and green tartan plaid Christmas tablecloth on the dining room table with a red table runner and candles. She and I place our mother's fancy earthenware dishes on the table. The dinner will be served buffet style. A sumptuous feast awaits the guests: "jug, jug," peas and rice, turkey, ham, and, of course, fried plantains.

About 15 minutes later, an entourage of guests files into the house. They are our neighbors and family members living in the New York area. A gust of cold, wintry wind blows in with each arrival. There are guffaws and peals of laughter as my parents are there to greet them. "Betty, so good to see you!" "Merry Christmas, Father Scantlebury!" the guests respond.

As the guests are seated in the living room, the hickory scent of the fireplace fills the air. Monica and I serve sorrel, while our mother serves the codfish cakes. Guests get up to help themselves to the main course followed by cassava pone, coconut bread, and "black cake." "Betty, do you remember when …." More stories ensue.

As the evening winds down, I anticipate what will come next … musical performance. No party is complete without a musical soirée. Sure enough, my mother announces, "Let's have some music! Joy, play that piece you have been working on." I go to the piano and play "Rink Queen", which I have memorized. It is my mother's favorite. Even though I am nervous playing in front of an audience, it is a pleasure to play in front of a friendly, supportive group. Monica plays "Take Me Back," a gospel song with robust chords, which she plays well. Then my father sits down on the piano bench and plays Christmas hymns as we all sing along. Some guests start harmonizing. When he starts to play the lesser-known Christmas hymn, "Christians, Awake! Salute the Happy Morn," my mother jumps up and announces, "This hymn takes me back to my childhood. We used to sing this hymn in Barbados!" She walks over to the piano and sings with gusto while my father accompanies her. A smile emerges on her face as she sings with all her heart and soul.

Nadia Giannopoulos

Nadia was born in the United States to parents of Greek origin. As a first-generation American, her parents instilled in her the importance of furthering one's education for self-growth and the opportunities it would afford. Her family, commitment to community service, and passion for education have remained at the forefront of her engagements, having led to volunteer opportunities within her local community and a passion for furthering her education. Nadia's undergraduate studies were focused on communication science, then two consecutive graduate degrees followed. She is currently a doctoral candidate at Vanderbilt University pursuing a degree in leadership. Nadia's experience as an educator lies both in and out of the classroom. Over the past 14 years, she has continued to serve as an executive director, overseeing all functions of a large and established special education program in Manhattan. Nadia resides in Long Island with her family. Her heritage takes precedence as she continues to visit her family in Greece with her children, ages 10 and 12 years, and works to incorporate the teachings into their after-school activities.

The author's grandparents, Konstantine and Efthalia, in their village in Greece with her beloved Kitso the goat

EXCERPT

The ability to travel to Europe for two months each year on very humble means allowed me the opportunity to be in touch with another side of life. I knew what struggle was, as it was a different struggle than an American one. I was a witness to a population who struggled financially, though they weren't depressed about it, nor did I ever pick up on it. They made it work and made their focal point about their family and more broadly their community. There was wisdom preserved, as these were generations who had lived through a difficult era, a continuous war. They knew how to behold what was important and cut through the noise. These memories and cultural roots ground me. Though I do get distracted at times, I find I can pivot to what's important, the importance of family, being loyal, and finding happiness within the simple moments all bound by love.

SECTION 2: Fond Childhood Memories of the Immigrant Community

Summers in Greece

[Greek]

Nadia Giannopoulos

As I approached the last day of school and heard the chatter of camp and summer plans, a wave of anticipation weighed heavily on me. I was the only child who wasn't "American" and even more strangely, was bilingual. Unlike the other children, I would not be around for playdates. Newark airport awaited my arrival as I would be shipped off to Greece, alone! I'm not even sure how ethical it was, but I was the only 7-year-old flying with an assigned flight attendant who would periodically check up on me. Upon arrival, I would be escorted to my extended family. Overall, I was an extremely quiet and obedient child, at times a select mute.

My suitcase was bigger than most, and not for reasons you would imagine. It was busting at the seams packed with the highly anticipated sheet sets my mom prepared as gifts annually for my father's siblings and grandparents in exchange for unloading me for the summer. For context, my father left his parents' home very young to work in Athens and then moved to America where he fell in love with my mother; he sparingly returned to the homeland. He was the handsome and beloved child that everyone admired and was well known. As his only child, my extended family was extremely attached to me. Though I wasn't the boy they were all praying for, I was his clone and was named Kostadina, the female derivative of his father's name, Konstantine; a Greek custom that is in order, the naming of your child after the paternal father.

Some people may imagine a European vacation as a luxury, but it was anything other than vacationing on the Mediterranean Riviera. My European vacation consisted of bouncing around to my father's sister's very humble apartment in Athens. His brother had a beach home north of Athens in the region of Marathon. Athens in the summer is not ideal; it is hot, noisy, and dusty. The highlight would come as we would near the end of the summer and drive to my grandparents' farm in a very far away village, the most northern peak of a mountain in Ioannina in the Epirus Region of Greece. Our village was named Mavropoulo, which translates into "blackbird."

At the time it was an eight-hour drive from Athens, which would take twists and turns along the edge of a mountain. Some junctures only allowed the passage of one car, and some turns would require holding your breath and saying a prayer. My grandparents were the first house on the right: a white, small, one-story stucco home with baby blue windows and baby blue shutters. Their home kicked off the village "block." It was customary upon arrival for my aunt to walk me to each home in the village (most of which were our relatives in some capacity). Before I left for my walk, my grandmother, Efthalia, would shove a whole garlic bulb in my pocket, which was barely hidden, to protect me from the evil eye. I didn't have a name, I was just "Tou Antoni h kori, aptin Amerikh" (Antonio's daughter from America). Everyone would kiss me and lovingly dissect me as though I was a foreign species, followed by sharing a story about a momentous memory they lived with my father. It was a meaningful shared experience in which I got to know my father through the lens of an outsider, with stories and memories that resonated with me.

My grandfather, Konstantine, and I were inseparable. We would spend time caring for the animals on his farm. I would accompany him on the late afternoon walks we would take before sunset, with his flock of sheep. On our walks, he would relive stories about my father's childhood and World War II in which my grandfather fought. The war spiraled into the Greek civil war which would cause further famine and devastation in what was left of Greece. I would learn all about my grandfather being stationed in Italy and Germany, and missing the opportunity to raise his children.

One summer, there was one goat I fell in love with named Kitso. He was a baby and all I would do is want to visit and care for him. He was *my goat*. On August 15, we would celebrate the feast day of the Virgin Mary. It is one of our largest Greek Orthodox holidays. It is an all-day affair that would last from morning into night. Families with roots in our village would fly in from all parts of Europe and would dance on church grounds to folk music ranging from clarinets to the bouzouki. Lamb and goat would be roasted, as per tradition, though I never really made the connection. What I learned years after my grandfather's passing, on a visit with my husband and 1-year-old son, was that my grandfather was supposed to make an offer for the festival that year but backed down. The baby goat that was meant to be sacrificed for the holiday was the one I had fallen in love with. Though I would never know, he couldn't commit to betraying me, not with Kitso or any of his goats. I cried so much when I found out, as it portrayed and instilled in me the deepest sense of loyalty and love.

The ability to travel to Europe for two months each year on very humble means allowed me the opportunity to be in touch with another side of life. I knew what struggle was, as it was a different struggle than an American one. I was a witness to a population who struggled financially, though they weren't depressed about it, nor did I ever pick up on it. They made it work and made their focal point about their family and more broadly their community. There was wisdom preserved, as these were generations who had lived through a difficult era, a continuous war. They knew how to behold what was important and cut through the noise. These memories and cultural roots ground me. Though I do get distracted at times, I find I can pivot to what's important, the importance of family, being loyal, and finding happiness within the simple moments all bound by love.

SECTION 2: Fond Childhood Memories of the Immigrant Community

3
The Immigrant Household and Food

Mamma Dina: Food as Love 53
   [Greek]
   Vicky Giouroukakis

The Culinary Cardinal 58
   [Italian]
   Maria C. Palmer

Rice Ball Stick Together 63
   [Taiwanese]
   Cindy (Ai-Ling) Li

First-Generation Persian-Jewish-American Family Thanksgivings and Blessings 67
   [Persian-Jewish]
   Rebecca Yousefzadeh Sassouni

Editor's Essay

EXCERPT

Mom was tiny, barely 5 ft 1 in, but rotund and buxom, and had the best posture for someone carrying all that weight. She walked like a coquette—the confident woman she was—and boasted to us that back in her village, everyone admired how she carried herself—that and her cleverness. Mom was tough, bold, and proud. Rumor has it that once when mom was little, she beat up a bunch of boys in school who called her an orphan. She waited for them after school and jumped them when they least expected it. My brothers and I believed it because we knew our mom wasn't afraid of anyone or anything and put the fear of God in us.

The author with (left to right) her mother-in-law, Anna, late mother, Constantina, and daughter, Anna, baking cookies for their church festival's bake sale in 2015

Mamma Dina: Food as Love

[Greek]

Vicky Giouroukakis

"Eat, eat," my mother, Dina, would say as if it was the manna from God. At family meals, which were mandatory on Sundays, she would be the last to sit at the dinner table and the last to put food on her plate, making sure everyone had more than enough to eat. Her hazel green eyes would quickly jump around from plate to plate and know exactly what and how much each of us consumed. If she wasn't satisfied with what she saw, she would call us out and urge us to finish our food. When we were little, mom would go to extremes by pretending to cry (she was very theatrical but also would cry at the drop of a dime, so we weren't sure what to believe). When we got older, she would resort to guilt and say, "It's not good to waste food." My father and two brothers, Steve and George, would acquiesce and clean their plates to appease her while I refused in protest of what I perceived to be an irrational and annoying demand.

Even years later when I was in postgraduate school, mom would try to impose her will on me, or at least that is how I interpreted it at the time. She would drive from New York to Philadelphia just to deliver bagels and Rome apples, my favorite, which I accepted with mixed emotions of appreciation and resentment. We would talk on the phone daily, and the second question she would ask after "How are you?" was "Have you eaten yet?" followed by "*What* did you eat?" I thought, *What was all the fuss about anyway?* When I was married and had my own home, mom would ask the same questions with the addition of "What did you cook today?" and "What did the kids eat?" By that point, I had learned to indulge her by answering her questions without getting annoyed.

Mom tried to feed or force feed (depending on how you look at it) the entire world—her relatives, friends, neighbors, doctors, and the mail carrier. One day, my aunt, Athanasia, came over unannounced, and mom insisted she cook dinner for her. My aunt protested that she had already eaten at her house. However, mom insisted, and before you knew it, she had defrosted a filet of sole, cooked it in oil, and served it piping hot in record time. She then watched my aunt eat every piece, beaming with pride. Now, whether it was my aunt's sense of obligation or her own desire to consume the food was irrelevant. The result is that it satiated mom.

Mom had the reputation of being an excellent cook. She would scribble recipes her own mother used or ones she got from cooking shows, friends, or relatives in a red marble notebook she kept securely in one of the kitchen drawers. You name the Greek dish and she made it—pastitsio (Greek lasagna), *makaronia* and *kima* (spaghetti with ground beef), *fasolakia* (green string beans), *fakes* (lentil soup), spanakopita (spinach pie), *tiropita* (cheese pie), and *bougatsa* (custard pie with phyllo). Our fridges, yes two fridges, were never empty, perhaps because they provided security that there would always be enough food.

Growing up, I considered food to be secondary to my reading as I much preferred the latter. Yet I was also intrigued and mystified by mom's cooking methods. I watched her methodically knead the dough, roll it out in thin sheets, stretch it out on pillows, make the spinach/feta cheese mixture, add it to the phyllo, roll it up, put it in an oiled pan, and bake it. And voila—delicious spinach pie! Mom made more than enough to feed our family AND the neighbors, AND to donate to the church for Sunday coffee hour.

Mom also loved to host, and people flocked to our house to sample her food and be nourished, indeed, to excess. She was the life of the party, always laughing and dancing, getting her guests to dance, and breaking plates until the wee hours of the morning. I learned to cook by watching mom do her magic in the kitchen and didn't realize it until years later when, as a newlywed, I had my own kitchen and surprised even myself by cooking my first meal from memory.

Mom was tiny, barely 5 ft 1 in, but rotund and buxom, and had the best posture for someone carrying all that weight. She walked like a coquette—the confident woman she was—and boasted to us that back in her village, everyone admired how she carried herself—that and her cleverness. Mom was tough, bold, and proud. Rumor has it that once when mom was little, she beat up a bunch of boys in school who called her an orphan. She waited for them after school and jumped them when they least expected it. My brothers and I believed it because we knew our mom wasn't afraid of anyone or anything and put the fear of God in us. Mom was also physically strong. When dad was at work, we would watch her single-handedly lift and move couches and beds into our new house. "Never depend on a man," she would say to me, not because mom resented dad, but because she believed that women should be independent and self-sufficient, which she felt was liberating.

Unlike mom who was bold and assertive, when we were younger, we were too shy and embarrassed to express what we wanted. At parties, we would nudge her to ask for a second round of hors d'oeuvres during cocktail hour or an extra bread roll at dinner. Mom would oblige with extreme pleasure to the point that in the absence of a request, she would anticipate it and carry it out anyway. "Oh, I brought you some extra shrimp that you like."

Perhaps mom's infatuation with food and eating was a result of her growing up in poverty. She was born in a tiny mountainous village in Corinth, Greece shortly after the German occupation of World War II and worked on the farm. Her father died when she was two years old, and her mother raised three children on her own, with some help from their relatives who took pity on them. Having little to eat, they made do with the basics—flour, olive oil, and lentils. Mom barely finished elementary school before she was forced to end her education so that she could work to support her family. Dad always said, and we all agreed, that if circumstances were different, she could have achieved professional success. When she and her siblings were older, they ended up in Athens, where they could find work and send money home. This is where mom met dad and got married.

Dad always told the story of how he first met mom and fell in love with her wit and resourcefulness. He was friends with some of her male relatives who tried to set him up with her. They decided one day to pay a visit to mom and her siblings at their home in Athens. Mom had no idea and came out of the shower in a robe and with a towel wrapped around her hair. She looked at the guests, greeted them, and as is customary in Greek culture, ran to the kitchen to take out some fruit and drinks to treat them. Realizing that she had no toothpicks for the fruit, she found a box of matches, broke off the points, and then stuck them in the fruit. As mom was serving the fruit, dad realized what she had done and smiled in amusement. She vivaciously proceeded to engage him in small talk and clever banter, and dad was impressed with how sharp she was. That was the beginning of their short courtship. Two months later, they were married.

After a few years, in 1969, my parents decided to move to the United States to pursue the American Dream. They ended up settling in Astoria, New York with no knowledge of the English language and no support. My father immediately began working at a Greek restaurant where he used many of mom's recipes. Mom would often go and help by putting her culinary expertise to good use. She made spinach and cheese pies, pastitsio, baklava, and *galaktoboureko*, among other Greek dishes.

Eventually, mom ended up working for several years at a watch factory which involved the tedious job of assembling watches but provided good employee benefits and salary. When my siblings and I were teenagers, mom decided to stay home for a few years to raise us. While dad worked long hours at the pizzeria, mom would take care of the house and always made sure to have a homecooked meal on the table for the family. She never expected us to help with the chores, as she wanted us to focus on our schooling and become educated and successful in life. As the one responsible for handling the money in the household, mom was economical. She made reasonable financial choices so that her children could live comfortably, while forgoing luxuries for herself. She saved money on food, monitoring supermarket sales, and tried not to let food go to waste. For example, even when she made fish, she used the unused parts to make soup.

Mom developed breast cancer later in life, and after receiving chemotherapy and radiation, was able to beat it and become cancer free for the next 20 years. Unfortunately, she was later diagnosed with lung cancer, which she fought for years. However, mom's cooking did not slow down; in fact, it accelerated and was as good. She even joined the cooking club at our church (a club that I started in mom's honor that offers cooking lessons to raise money for the poor) and served as guest chef a few times. In the last two years before she passed away, when mom was unable to cook, dad took over and cooked her favorite recipes. Even illness could not take down her vivacious personality and sense of humor as she would often joke and complain to dad that her cooking was better, even though she knew very well that his was just as good.

Over the years, mom learned enough English to be able to function in society, but when she had to talk to doctors and medical staff, she struggled to communicate with them. She asked my brothers and me to serve as translators and advocates on her behalf, partly because of the language barrier and partly because she wanted our company. Mom compensated for her lack of English by cooking Greek delicacies for the doctors, nurses, and receptionists, even when she became very ill and weak. This was her way of showing them an appreciation for taking care of her. She would deliver the food during her visits, always with a smile on her face and emotional tears in her eyes, gestures that endeared the staff.

Years after I had left her house, I realized that mom's preoccupation with food and eating had to do with her desire to take care of her family and loved ones in the one way that she knew best, by cooking for and feeding us—this was her way of controlling her life and her situation. Mom had no education, literacy, hobbies, or financial means. And she lacked language, so whatever she could not communicate in English she could communicate using the silent message of food. Food was the medium through which she conveyed her love toward people, her family, and the whole world.

Maria Costanzo Palmer

Maria Costanzo Palmer grew up in Pittsburgh, PA, in an Italian-American family. Even though all her Italian-born relatives have passed, she continues to embrace both cultures.

She is a writer and Page Turner Award Finalist for her debut book *On the Rocks* (August 8, 2023), a book about the rise and fall of her award-winning restaurateur father. She has vast experience working in the non-profit world for *Get on the Bus*, a nonprofit dedicated to uniting children with their incarcerated parents. Maria is currently a grant writer for St. Paul's Development Corporation.

The author with her daughters

EXCERPT

But the room was perfect for my grandma's elaborate cooking endeavors. It was the ideal space for her to be able to teach us the value of what being Italian really meant. Although we were all born in America, you wouldn't know it because of our exposure to the food of our homeland. She used this little kitchen to cook the magic of homemade sauce making, sausage stuffing, and pasta rolling. Once it was all over, the garden hose and within a flash, all the evidence disappeared.

The Culinary Cardinal

[Italian]

Maria C. Palmer

    I walked into my grandparents' unfinished basement, which doubled as my Italian grandma's cellar kitchen. Her cooking mecca was made only of cement with a series of exposed pipes lining the walls, which jutted out and created a maze effect throughout. There was a drain in the center of the room for easy clean up. The only natural light came through a glass block window keeping the room dark and dreary even on the brightest days. The standing joke was that if someone was unfamiliar with the space, it could be mistaken for the setting of a serial killer movie. But the room was perfect for my grandma's elaborate cooking endeavors. It was the ideal space for her to be able to teach us the value of what being Italian really meant. Although we were all born in America, you wouldn't know it because of our exposure to the food of our homeland. She used this little kitchen to cook the magic of homemade sauce making, sausage stuffing, and pasta rolling. Once it was all over, the garden hose and within a flash, all the evidence disappeared.

    Steam escaped as hints of marinara sauce hit my nose. I inhaled the aromas of sauteed garlic, onion, basil, parsley, and ripe off-the-vine tomatoes that were slowly simmering on the stove. I began to salivate. The heat fogged my glasses. I spotted my grandma guarding watch over a steel-covered stock pot as she dipped her wooden spoon into her deep red marinara sauce. She slowly stirred the pot of liquid ecstasy to make sure it cooked evenly. She took a quick break and shifted her focus to an adjacent large pot of water, turning the heat on high. My arrival was timed perfectly as she was in between finishing one dish and starting the next. I hugged my grandma and more hints of our future meal emerged. Her hands were dusted with leftover flour and made handprints on my black shirt. The aroma of a hard Italian cheese that she likely spent the morning grating was around. To her left was a fold up table that she used as her prep table. On it, I saw ground beef, cheese, breadcrumbs, and eggs—ingredients for my favorite dish—*polpettes*, Italian fried meatballs. I knew I was in for a treat.

    After a brief greeting, I knew that I needed to now make myself invisible until dinner because when grandma was cooking, no one should ever interrupt or question her. This was one of the unspoken rules growing up Italian that we all obeyed.

    While my other cousins ran out to play, I stayed behind. My grandma allowed me to sit quietly as I watched and learned on a stool from a distance. Although I wouldn't get a formal cooking lesson from my grandma until many years later, watching her in action taught me more than I had ever realized.

Watching her make the *polpettes* was like watching a conductor start a symphony. She used her large mixing bowl to call every ingredient one by one by instinct. She started with the ground meat base and then took a handful of cheese followed by a handful of breadcrumbs. She took apart the parsley sprigs one by one, and they took a dive into the mixture. Lastly, she added an egg and then mixed it by hand. She felt the mixture with her eyes closed, searching for the familiar, and doctored it as needed. This time, she added another egg and some more cheese.

When she was satisfied, she put oil in her sauté pan and turned the heat on. She reached into the mixing bowl and pulled out a palm-sized amount of meat. She rolled the mixture in between her hands quickly back-and-forth three times to create meatballs in the shape of logs. She ripped a piece of bread and threw it into the sauté pan to make sure the oil was hot enough. The sharp crackle as the crispy bread rose to the top meant it was ready. The *polpettes* nestled in the hot oil lined up one by one into the hot oil. Watching closely, she used two forks to rotate each *polpette*, equally browning all sides to create the perfect crunch. She wiped the sweat off her face with her apron.

My skin glistened from the oil-heavy air. The meatballs sizzled off the pan. My eyes felt heavy, and my stomach felt hungry. I wanted a bite. I prayed that she needed to step away to use the bathroom or that she accidentally had some leftover ingredients that were not enough to make a full *polpette*. As a reward for my patience, my grandma gave me a taste on the sly. This was our secret not to be shared with anyone else. I was willing to sacrifice burning my tongue by biting into a newly fried *polpette*. The taste of the crunch on the outside and the wild burst of tenderness on the inside would be well worth it.

I wanted her to teach me how to cook step-by-step, like the cooking shows on television, but she never did. When I tried to ask her a question about what she was doing, she told me to "wait a while" until she was able to finish. She was not one for words or explanations. When I asked her how she knew that the *polpettes* were done cooking, she just shrugged and offered me a small piece. I gladly accepted. No matter how annoyed I felt by not being answered, all was easily forgiven with the taste of her meatballs. After the newly cooked *polpettes* landed on the plate, she dropped the homemade pasta in the piping hot water. She took a break and quickly ran to the bottom of the staircase. She yelled, "Ready!" before running back to her pasta pot to make sure her noodles were cooking to al dente perfection.

Within seconds, soldiers of hungry aunts and uncles came down. She passed platters of piping hot food to each person, who in turn marched the food up the steps to the main dining room.

After the final entrée was plated, we all sat down in a small dining room with a makeshift table too large to accommodate the space comfortably, but just large enough for all of us. Once I was in my seat, I was stuck, and eating was now the only option. Oh, how I loved Sundays!

Grandma's seat was the only exception. She sat in a chair by the kitchen and was the only person who was able to get up during the meal. She surveyed the room to make sure everyone had what they needed. She effortlessly went between the kitchen and dining room delivering extra sauce, grated cheese, and coarse ground pepper. This was how she showed her love and devotion to the family.

My grandfather yelled "Sparrow!" Sparrow was a nickname my grandfather gave my grandma as she reminded him of a little bird quickly and effortlessly feeding her flock. He was the only person who could get her to come in and sit down with the family. As she started to fill her plate with samples of all the food she prepared, she still had her apron on as she wiped the sweat away from her brow. She took a taste of everything but never indulged the way that the rest of us did.

Years later, when grandma finally agreed to give me a cooking lesson, I learned why she hadn't eaten so much. She was tasting all along to make sure the combination of the ingredients was exactly right. If not, like a chemist, she was able to alter on the fly to bring flavors more alive by adding spices, cutting back on thick sauces with water, and adding more flour to dough that was just too sticky to work with. However, whenever I questioned her about when to employ what tactic, I always got the same answer, "You just know what to do because you've done it so long."

Grandma also was particular about how the ingredients were prepared. She allowed me to help chop an onion for her sauce and when she looked over and saw me traditionally dicing it on a cutting board, she stopped me and said, "You are doing this all wrong." Without flinching, she picked up what was left of my abused onion and held it in her hand and started slicing it freehand, making small slits longways pulling the knife toward her. Then she shifted the onion in her hand and ran the knife perpendicular using her thumb as a guide to make perfect cubes of onion which went right into the pot. I had my doubts of how you could cut an onion all wrong, but after watching how she did it, I understood.

She died suddenly right after Christmas when I was newly married. Almost immediately, a cardinal appeared at my kitchen window. It showed up during the times that I was cooking and mostly trying to recreate the Italian dishes I grew up on. When the cardinal came, it never stayed long. It never made direct eye contact with me and when I tried to take a photo, it flew away. I laughed at the irony because for years, my grandmother straddled both the Italian and American cultures. She never quite fit into either, so she was a quiet observer of both. She was a woman of few words, but when she felt strongly about something like cooking, she made her point known.

Over the years, little by little, I was able to bring some dishes back that had circulated off the menu when my grandma died. I recognized the culinary energy of repetition, and I started to feel what I needed to do. A concept that was foreign years before had taken root in my life. And through this time, when I was cooking my grandma's recipes, the cardinal kept showing up.

Years later, I wanted my first child Helena, named after my grandma, to cook with me. She was five years old at the time, and this was not her first culinary rodeo. I had her assist me in mixing dough for the ricotta gnocchi we were going to eat for Christmas Eve. We watched refresher videos of my grandma making food before diving in. We mixed the ricotta, eggs, Romano cheese, and flour mixture together. We transferred our conglomeration of ingredients to a cutting board and started cutting 2-in slices from the ball of ingredients. We rolled each out like a snake and cut each on a bias. We then coated each one with a sprinkle of flour and rolled them with our thumb on a fork to create divots on the outer edge of each individual gnocchi pillow.

As I was in process, my daughter said loudly, "Mommy, you are doing it all wrong." Words that sounded all too familiar. I stopped and gazed out the window and in my bush was a beautiful cardinal staring back at me. At that moment, three generations of culinary excellence had coincided. My heart warmed within as I wiped the tears away and hugged little Helena.

Cindy (Ai-Ling) Li

Cindy (Ai-Ling) Li and her family immigrated to the United States when she was only seven years old. Despite her status in the States, she has always been passionate about advocating for Asians and Asian Americans, which brought her down the path of education. She received her bachelor's degree in child development with a multiple subject credential and added Mandarin Bilingual Authorization in 2016. She has taught in the public school setting as a primary Mandarin dual-language teacher for six years. She received her master's degree in education with an emphasis on reading and literacy. She received her Reading Specialist Credential along with a Reading Added Authorization with the completion of her studies in the master's program. Her main employment is at Pacific Oaks College in Pasadena, California as a core faculty member in the School of Human Development and Education and as a specialist on the Bilingual Authorization Program to further educate interested teacher candidates on the beauty of dual-language education and how to bring the culture and traditions of the Asian language to students and families.

The author

EXCERPT

In the Asian culture, rice has been a staple food item in which other entrées may be served in alignment to the "star" of the show. No matter what entrées may be served on the table (vegetable dish, meat dish, seafood dish, or a soup), rice will always be the center of attention and has to be served on the table while eating. Rice is what keeps the ingredients cohesive, and oftentimes, when I think of my family, I think of us as being very similar to the rice in rice balls, as we had to "stick together" in order to create our own cohesive family unit. I enjoyed eating rice balls until one particular incident occurred that almost made me throw away my entire culture and identity.

Rice Balls Stick Together

[Taiwanese]

Cindy (Ai-Ling) Li

In the Asian culture, rice has been a staple food item in which other entrées may be served in alignment to the "star" of the show. No matter what entrées may be served on the table (vegetable dish, meat dish, seafood dish, or a soup), rice will always be the center of attention and has to be served on the table while eating. There are also many alternate ways to use rice, especially in cooking, such as in a liquid-type form to make a porridge-type food or mashing rice into a powderlike substance to make sweet dessert items like mochi. One may even wrap items such as fish, long vegetables, ginger, and many other items inside of rice; that is what a rice ball is. However, in order to keep the other ingredients inside the rice ball, the rice has to have a sufficient sticky consistency and be compressed tight enough in order to keep the other ingredients inside. Rice is what keeps the ingredients cohesive, and oftentimes, when I think of my family, I think of us as being very similar to the rice in rice balls, as we had to "stick together" in order to create our own cohesive family unit. I enjoyed eating rice balls until one particular incident occurred that almost made me throw away my entire culture and identity.

Once, my mother had packed rice balls made of sushi rice and tuna. A vast difference between sushi rice and regular rice is that sushi rice has a white vinegar component added when making the rice, so there could be a sour smell when freshly made; however, it is the sour consistency of the sushi rice that makes the other components of the rice ball—tuna, mayonnaise, and seaweed—so delicious. It was that one morning on which my mother had made sushi rice balls and had my brothers and I bring it to school to eat. When it came to mealtime at school, my brothers and I excitedly unpacked our bags and brought our sushi rice balls out to munch away on. However, to our horror, the students sitting around us started pinching their noses. They asked with disgust, "Eew! What is that smell?" At that time, although my brothers and I didn't completely understand their language since there was a language barrier, we understood their body language. And we were embarrassed.

We tried our best to wolf down our sushi rice balls down our throats to decrease the laughter and fingers being pointed at us. However, one of my brothers was already not feeling well that daunting morning, so in wolfing down his sushi rice ball, the sour taste didn't sit well in his digestive system, and the next thing we knew, his food regurgitated back up his throat … and onto the table. There was even more disgust from the classmates around us as the cafeteria became rowdy and panicked. The teacher monitoring the cafeteria came to see what the noise was about and quickly escorted my brother to the nurse's office. From that incident on, along with the language barrier, it became very difficult for my brothers and me to establish friends at the school. For quite some time, my brothers and I had to rely on one another to become our own companions at this foreign and, in our opinion, "judgmental school." Luckily, after some time, we all transferred to another school and, eventually, started to make a few friends outside of our sibling group.

After that horrifying incident, for a very long time, I learned to be cautious when eating rice balls or even other Chinese foods at school. To me, the idea of eating rice balls at school was terrifying since I didn't know what kind of discrimination I was going to face. I rejected the idea of eating rice balls and other food my mother packed and what it stood for. There also was a drift between my siblings, myself, and my parents as my siblings and I assimilated more and more to the "American" culture and lost sight of our original "identity" as Taiwanese immigrants. However, it wasn't until my mother tried to teach me how to make rice balls that I started to see the value of rice balls and the importance of one food item in a culture.

As my mother tightly squeezed the rice around the other ingredients inside the rice ball, she started to explain that in order to make a cohesive rice ball, the rice must have enough of a sticky consistency to stick together; however, the grip of the hands, when mashing the rice together, must also be firm enough to make the rice stick to the other ingredients. She compared the rice to our family structure; one's family members must always "stick together" and work with one another in order to have tightened rice around the other ingredients and make a delicious rice ball. She also described the grip of the hands as a "resistance" to outside noises; if one's resolve is not strong enough, then one would not be able to squeeze the rice together to make a cohesive rice ball. It made me see rice balls, and other Chinese food, in a very different light. I remembered that we, as a family of six immigrants, had to rely on either extended family members or friends in order to survive for some time, since we did not have any immediate family in the United States. Otherwise, in order to establish our independence and avoid relying on others' support, my mother and father had to find manual labor jobs that were grueling, since the certifications and training they had in Taiwan didn't transfer to America.

For a long period of time, my mother had to remain the stay-at-home mother to take care of the house, and my father had learned a business trade (contracting) to make a livable wage for his family. We learned that anything that we wanted, we had to earn on our own. However, regardless of the things I couldn't buy or own as a child, one aspect that I really looked forward to was my mother's cooking. She learned to make delicious food for our family, such as rice balls, typically served in the morning. Breakfast was my favorite time of the day, since it was the first meal I woke up to, and the delicious aroma of freshly packed rice balls was certainly one way to wake me up. Although breakfast in my household was very much a "grab and go" style, since family members were always rushing to either school or work in the mornings, having the warmth of fresh rice in my hands as I was eating on the way to school reminded me of my mother's warmth and love that she put into the rice ball.

    I realized then that my resolve in embracing my original identity wasn't enough. I had almost let myself "crumble"—like when rice isn't sticky enough and could crumble under pressure—and succumb to the "American" culture and ways, since I was embarrassed of my background, my failings, and my lack of awareness at school. I learned that I had to strengthen my identity and resolve as being an educated Asian American immigrant who may eat American food, like burgers and fries, but will also eat Chinese food, like rice balls. I embraced a new identity in myself: I am educated, I am a woman, and I am a colored second-generation immigrant. I also embraced a new passion in life, as I would like to advocate for Asian Americans, especially immigrants, who might have faced the same discrimination as I did once upon a time. I want them to proudly eat their rice balls (or any other Chinese foods) in public without any scrutiny. Most importantly, post pandemic, I would like to provide a voice to Asian American immigrants, like myself, and remind the world that we all need to "stick together" to create a brighter and more cohesive future for Asian Americans. Maybe then, we could all sit down together at a table and eat a delicious meal with rice balls together.

Rebecca Yousefzadeh Sassouni

Rebecca Yousefzadeh Sassouni is a first-generation American, first-born daughter of Iranian Jewish immigrants from Iran. Rebecca is a lawyer, mediator, writer, seeker, and intermittent faster. Her relationship to cuisine and cooking is deeply tethered to her relationships to her religion (Judaism), her ethnicity (Persian), and her gender (cis female) and to her identities as a wife, mother, daughter, daughter-in-law, mother-in-law, sister, cousin, aunt, and friend. Rebecca cooks to gather loved ones close in the tradition of the millennia of matriarchs before her.

EXCERPT

The author with her family in her kitchen

On Thanksgiving (which this year coincided with Rosh Chodesh Kislev, the beginning of a lunar month including Hanukkah), we came together in my home to enjoy not only a delicious meal but a collective wish for all homes and hearts to be sated, for integration and peace among the generations and the ethnicities, cultures, and religions, and good health for all.

First-Generation Persian-Jewish-American Family Thanksgivings and Blessings

[Persian-Jewish]

Rebecca Yousefzadeh Sassouni

I was born in the United States and grew up in the 1970s with the whole "Pilgrim" and "Indian" narrative of Thanksgiving, followed by its debunking and replacement with the colonial pillage narrative, but, to be honest, I never really appreciated the holiday itself much until my own children grew up and went away to college.

You see, as a child and young adult, I was not permitted to dorm, and my family kept Shabbat on Fridays until sundown on Saturdays, so Thanksgiving dinner felt more like two nights in a row of delicious, authentic, home-cooked Persian Shabbat dinner, plus poultry (love you, Mom).

Don't get me wrong: We got together, and I was really lucky in that respect. My family did both the secular holiday of Thanksgiving on the third Thursday in November and the Jewish weekly observance of Shabbat. I grew up with both, and I just didn't know enough to be grateful for that back then. Many immigrant families at the time would have had either-or. Mine, ever adaptive and educable, tried for both, even if our Thanksgiving meant turkey, not necessarily stuffing, cranberry sauce, or pies ….

Now, years later, I look back at my immigrant parents, grandparents, and in-laws to marvel at their adaptations with tremendous admiration. As an American parent myself now, with children who have grown and who do live away from home, I finally appreciate the sweetness of this Thanksgiving gathering every year. I look forward with eagerness for weeks to seeing our children around the table (including via Zoom!) and appreciate the gathering of the generations of our family more with each passing year.

In the intervening years since my childhood, my own family has become increasingly divided in its observance of Shabbat. Some no longer travel in vehicles on Fridays and Saturdays. It turns out that Thanksgiving, always on Thursday, provides a secular touchstone to avoid issues of competing Jewish observances.

Last year, at this time, our eldest was engaged and we invited our *machetonim* (a Yiddish word I learned for one's child's in-laws). They had suffered the devastating loss of their patriarch the night before Thanksgiving. We ended up sending one of the turkeys I had made over as a shiva meal. In a bittersweet manner, we were able to establish family roots around food and tradition precisely because we were apart, in their grief.

This year, *IYH* (Im Yirtze HaShem, Hebrew for With God's will), would be our first Thanksgiving with our children and parents, and the *machetonim* together. As I strove to integrate traditions to create purpose and meaning, over the last few weeks, I asked my indulgent, amazing, tender parents and teachers to teach me the recipes for some of the rarer Persian foods I had not yet learned to make over the years. My parents indulged me with their authentic insider Kashi-Tehrani scoops on how to make *Ash Anar* and *Gondi Berengee* which I will serve along with Persian jeweled rice as well as stuffing and veggies, and, of course, a giant turkey, and several pies. *Ash Anar* and *Gondi Berengee* came to mind as two comfort foods appropriate for the autumn season, rich with texture and fragrant with fruits and spices such as dried lemon, pomegranate, parsley, fenugreek, apricots, beets, chives, and more. We spent several hours together chopping, reminiscing, bickering, and laughing about the recipes and whose mother's was most authentic.

On Thanksgiving (which this year coincided with Rosh Chodesh Kislev, the beginning of a lunar month including Hanukkah), we came together in my home to enjoy not only a delicious meal but a collective wish for all homes and hearts to be sated, for integration and peace among the generations and the ethnicities, cultures, and religions, and good health for all.

4 Life Lessons Learned from Immigrant Parents

A Letter of Gratitude 71
   [Irish]
   Maggie Blair

The Values Instilled in Me by My Parents 75
   [Ghanaian]
   Gloria Serwa Gyimah

My Parents' Ultimate Sacrifice 79
   [Greek]
   Fiffy Eliades

Practicality 83
   [Irish]
   Noreen Williams

Ode to Glendita 87
   [Honduran]
   Ashley Tavormina

Better than a Thousand Sons 90
   [Indian]
   Mubina Schroeder

Guidance from a Guyanese Mother 94
   [Guyanese]
   Nadia Khan-Roopnarine

Mother and Children Discuss Immigrant Experiences 99
   [Jamaican]
   Sherone Smith-Sánchez and Her Children

Maggie Blair

Maggie Blair is the daughter of Florence Clarke and William P. Grier, both of whom left Ireland and immigrated to New York City in the 1930s. They met in New York and married in 1942 just before Bill left for Europe to serve in the U.S. Army under General George Patton. Upon his return, they bought a house and raised their family in the Clason Point section of the Bronx. Professionally, Maggie has spent 50+ years working in special education as a classroom teacher, a staff developer, and administrator. In the spring of 2020, she formally retired from Molloy University as an assistant professor but has remained on campus to establish the Molloy Opportunity for Successful Transition (MOST) Program, a three-year college experience that prepares developmentally delayed young adults to transition into the world of employment and community engagement.

The author

EXCERPT

After some thoughtful reflection on my memories of growing up in an immigrant family, I began to realize the debt of gratitude that I owed to my parents. Therefore, my reflection will take the form of a thank-you letter to my parents, Florence and Bill Grier.

A Letter of Gratitude

[Irish]

Maggie Blair

After some thoughtful reflection on my memories of growing up in an immigrant family, I began to realize the debt of gratitude that I owed to my parents. Therefore, my reflection will take the form of a thank-you letter to my parents, Florence and Bill Grier.

Dear Mom and Dad,

A dear colleague of mine recently embarked on a very interesting journey and along the way, she invited some friends to join her. When she posed her request for her newest publication, a personal reflection of my memories growing up in an immigrate family, I had mixed thoughts: This could be an enriching experience for me personally and a challenging endeavor for me professionally. Both outcomes have proven to be true.

As memories flooded back, three words consistently dominated my memories: faith, high expectations, and education. Over the past few months, I have watched the Ukrainians struggle to regain their sovereignty, their dignity, and their inherent freedoms. I am always saddened by the hardships faced by children in war-torn lands and think back to both of you, school-age children, during the years of the Irish Uprising, trying to make sense of your embattled homeland. I know that a deep sense of faith in the power of prayer carried your families through many long and trying days, weeks, and months. This is one of the most important gifts that you both gave to your family. I always subscribed to the "where," "when," and "how" prayer exercised during childhood and took my faith in the power of prayer with me through life. Thank you!

Some families talk incessantly and say barely anything of meaning. Other families say little—yet say so much!

My memories of you, Dad, were those of "the quiet man." You said little but had a formidable impact on so much of everything. When asked a question, you preferred not to answer. You would simply say, "Don't go away mad; just go!" You definitely answered the question asked—in your time and in your way—but you never opened a door that welcomed an argument! You were more a doer than a speaker. Your limited access to higher education and your immigrant status forced you to reflect on your personal strengths, to foster believe in yourself, and to raise your expectations for "success" in this new world. To accomplish these goals, you focused your attention on your immediate community, a small outlier tucked in the northeast corner of the Bronx.

You challenged yourself to reach personal success by generously spending endless hours of service to your local parish. You doggedly committed to your place of employment. By sharing your innate athletic skills and genuine kindness to the local neighborhood children, you worked with anyone who asked until they successfully passed the driver's test. You gave many of the young men employment opportunities, and you spent time coaching/umpiring stickball games with them on the corner, while never having played stickball before coming to the United States! Thank you for showing me what I can accomplish, if I successfully identify my talents and use them for the betterment of my community!

Mom, while you were the chief disciplinarian, you were also a quiet voice … quiet BUT when you had a plan, you were definitely a force to be reckoned with! Without ever saying a word, each of your three children ALWAYS knew that higher education and impactful careers were in our futures. Being the oldest of the trio and probably the most challenging to raise, I must thank you today for your insight, resourcefulness, and quiet determination when I decided not to return to college in my sophomore year. Without your presence in my life at that time, I would never have this opportunity to reflect on my amazing upbringing and be able to thank you for your courage and support. You raised me to discover who I am but more importantly, who I could be, or, rather, who I NEEDED to become …. Without saying a word, I learned from you the critical importance of setting and achieving high personal and professional expectations and always taking pride in myself and my accomplishments. You would frequently remind me that: "If you are going to take on a job, do it to the very best of your ability because that body of work reflects who you are!" This is a lesson I hope I successfully passed onto my own boys. Thank you for your patience and your fortitude as I searched for my personal talents and eventually used them to improve a small piece of the world.

Mom, while "wasting time on the telephone" was not one of your favorite pastimes, you always did enjoy a good conversation over tea with your two sisters who also came to the United States in the late 1920s and early 1930s. All three of you placed an extraordinarily high value on education as the key to future success. Frequently, these conversations focused on your children's success in the classroom. There were times when these conversations could get a bit competitive. The ultimate outcome of these "sisterly" conversations, however, was the success at which your combined nine children completed their educational journeys: Eight of the nine completed four years of college; seven of the nine completed a master's degree or above; and three of the nine went on to complete doctoral degrees or medical degrees! All went on to be successful in their chosen professions. While only seven of us are still alive, we remain close despite the implicit, maternal competition because we also shared those common values taught and nurtured by the three sisters. Thank you!

As I end this missive, I want to thank you both for having the courage, resilience, and determination to leave your family and the place you called "home" to create a new safe haven in a new country for your new family. When you arrived here, you brought with you little more than a deep faith in the power of prayer, an unbending conviction that both personal and professional standards of excellence must never be compromised, and the belief that education is unquestionably the key to personal and professional success. Thank you for all you taught me!

Gloria Serwa Gyimah

Gloria Serwa Gyimah lives in the Bronx, New York. She is an adjunct professor at Monroe College where she teaches in the School of Business, the Accounting Department, and in the School of Social Sciences. She has a bachelor's degree in general studies (focus in education) and two master's degrees in management: one in organizational leadership and the other in public administration. She is currently working on her doctorate in education, specifically in Curriculum, Instruction, and Assessment. She is an independent consultant for Paparazzi, selling jewelry. When she is not teaching, she is working as a vendor, spending time with family, reading, and participating in church activities. She is one busy lady, but God has given her the grace for the next level.

The author

EXCERPT

You would think that now that my parents are in a different country, they will adapt and follow the system of America. That is not what happened at all. Their Ghanaian mentality also migrated along with them. My parents are disciplinarians, especially my father. My siblings and I were raised to be God-fearing and respectful. Respect was an important feature in our household.

The Values Instilled in Me by My Parents

[Ghanaian]

Gloria Serwa Gyimah

Having immigrant parents can be quite interesting, quite unique, yet challenging but also very rewarding. My siblings and I were born in America, and we have the opportunity of having the best of both worlds.

Fun fact: my father, Yaw Ofosu, migrated to America from Ghana, West Africa 40 years ago! He came to pursue the "American Dream." He became friends with my grandfather (my mother's father) and became roommates.

This is how the story of the best of both worlds begins. My grandfather introduces his daughter (my mother, Yaa Owusua) to my father. As the saying goes, the rest of the story is history. At the time, my mother was in Ghana. My father did all the necessary marital customary rites in Ghana. My mother relocated to America the year after. The following year, they welcomed their first child, which is me. I am the only girl. I have two younger brothers.

My parents were both in agreement to work hard to fulfill and pursue the "American Dream." In those days, the American Dream was to work hard and make money, send money or resources to help the family back home so that they can live better, and build a house with the intention to retire and enjoy life to the fullest in Ghana. My parents came to America with only two suitcases and no money.

My father worked as a senior cook in the Department of Corrections, and my mother went to school to obtain her associate's and bachelor's degrees in nursing. She currently has a master's in public health.

You would think that now that my parents are in a different country, they will adapt and follow the system of America. That is not what happened at all. Their Ghanaian mentality also migrated along with them. My parents are disciplinarians, especially my father. My siblings and I were raised to be God-fearing and respectful. Respect was an important feature in our household. My father always says, "I do not want anyone (especially in the Ghanaian community) to say that my children are rude or not well-mannered. It makes me look bad as a father."

This statement was quite challenging to live by because here we were, my siblings and I, living in New York, the Bronx to be precise, in a nice and quiet environment where everyone kept to themselves. My siblings and I were going to school and working with people that did not have the same family dynamics that we were fortunate to have. I have heard so many stories of how people disrespect their parents, hurting their feelings by yelling and cussing at them when their parents did something that they did not like. There were people that we encountered that were coming from broken homes or blended families. My siblings and I never experienced that. We have always had both parents, who are still married, in our lives, so we are a very close-knit family.

That was not the situation in my household. If my parents did something that we did not agree upon, we kept quiet and would cry about it in our rooms. This treatment made my siblings and me very timid at times. We were always afraid to speak up or give our input about a topic that was being discussed. One thing that I struggle with to this day is to not disappoint my parents. We always wanted to accomplish so much to make our parents proud of us. What was more than gold for an African parent was to see their children succeed.

There are many examples or instances on how I struggled living with two cultures in one country. For example, my parents wanted me to become a nurse or to work in the medical field. I knew at the age of four years that I wanted to be an educator. It was a profession that runs in the family. My maternal grandfather and grandmother were both educators in Ghana. My mother was also an educator before she relocated to America. They were against me going to school to obtain a degree in education because they felt that educators do not make much money, and they are looked down on. My parents did all they can do to advise me to investigate another field. I had many family members and family friends speak to me about changing my career.

My goal and motivation were to prove to my parents that I will become a successful educator. I am proud to say that I am almost done with obtaining a doctorate degree, and I am currently working as a professor at Monroe College in New Rochelle.

My mother always says: "If I came from Ghana and went to school in America and obtained degrees, there is no excuse why you should not go to school and obtain degrees as well. I was born and raised in the village. I have worked hard. You guys are fortunate to be born here and have the American accent. Nothing should stop you from going to school and getting great jobs. You can make it, if you put your mind to it."

My parents demonstrated hardworking and persistent traits to us. I have helped develop leadership in others by serving as an example of how far you can go in education with dedication and hard work. By being a student, I have been an example to others who did not feel they could juggle working, going to school, and extracurricular activities. At the Church of Pentecost, Delaware Branch, I have served as the district youth leader for five years where I exercise dynamic leadership ability. I have a hardworking and decisive character that has brought me this far in life.

My family has faced many challenges like every family does—losing loved ones, getting laid off, misunderstandings, and so on—but one thing that holds our family together is our faith in God. I grew up in a Christian home where the Christian values was implemented in every area of our lives. My siblings and I are very active in our Church community. This helps us to enhance our faith and to put our trust in God and no one else. Being a child of an immigrant comes with a lot of challenges, but I would never trade the morals and values that were instilled in us.

Fiffy L. Eliades

Fiffy L. Eliades is married to her high school sweetheart, Dr. William Eliades, and they have two daughters. Marissa is a lawyer practicing in NYC, and Samantha, who was born with a rare syndrome, lives in a group home. At a young age, they moved to Roslyn, New York where they still reside. She graduated from Bernard Baruch College (CUNY) with a BBA and worked in the computer industry in NYC for many years. After having children, she has focused on helping her husband build his dental practices in Queens. Currently, Fiffy is committed to special-needs advocacy work and church-affiliated involvement, including being a Philoptochos (philanthropic church ministry) board member and a Parish Council board member.

The author with her parents, Despina and Serafim Liapis, and her brother, Gus

EXCERPT

My parents were anything but ordinary. My father, Serafim Liapis, was a loving husband, father, grandfather, brother, uncle, relative, and friend to all who knew him here and in Greece. Since his arrival to America, my father committed every day to his hard work as a chef at a family-run diner in Manhattan. His hard work never went unnoticed, and, unfortunately, it was where he saw his demise.

My Parents' Ultimate Sacrifice

[Greek]

Fiffy L. Eliades

This is a story of two people that worked so hard to provide for their family and to achieve the American Dream, while keeping their faith. As I get older, I reflect on how much I have been through and endured throughout my life. I think about how my perseverance is attributed to my family, faith, and the sacrifices my parents made to build a beautiful life for their family.

My parents were anything but ordinary. My father, Serafim Liapis, was a loving husband, father, grandfather, brother, uncle, relative, and friend to all who knew him here and in Greece. Since his arrival to America, my father committed every day to his hard work as a chef at a family-run diner in Manhattan. His hard work never went unnoticed, and, unfortunately, it was where he saw his demise. My father was stabbed to death on August 22, 1988, in a robbery in his place of work by a colleague who was desperate for money. The years following his death truly felt like a nightmare because we ironically lost the person who led our family here for a better life. He was mourned by so many and is missed every day.

Even now, so many years later, it makes no sense why my father died, and there are no words to express the pain suffered by those that knew him and loved him most. He was the most loving, generous man I have ever known, and I thank him for the love and commitment to his family. He taught us to love thy neighbor and to treat others how you want to be treated. My father made us laugh, showed us how to work hard, and most importantly, taught us to love family and friends unconditionally. A fond memory I have of my father that demonstrates these qualities was when he worked tirelessly to earn money to buy me a piano, when we definitely could not afford one. He was committed to getting me a piano so I could learn a new skill and practice current music to make me feel like a true American. He would frequently play Greek records and dance the *tsamiko* (a traditional folk dance) as a family, so I would never forget where I came from. He was the true meaning of the word *philotimos* (Greek; lover of honor). His death will always remain a blurry memory, but his life will always be a vivid one, the epitome of greatness and sacrifice.

My mom, Despina Liapis, dedicated her life to her family and being the best mom, sister, aunt, and *yiayia*. My mom was kind, loving, funny, simple, but fiercely loyal. After the passing of my father, she wore black every single day and committed her life to finding joy in family dinners, spending time with her children, attending her grandchildren's dance recitals, Greek school presentations, and school graduations. Most notably, she found joy watching *Jeopardy* every night despite not speaking a word of English. She was from Mikro Horio (literal translation is Small Village), Greece, where she met and married my father in an arranged marriage. After they married, they relocated to Athens and had a son, my brother Gus.

My family struggled in Greece and yearned for a better life for themselves and their growing family, and they were ultimately sponsored by relatives, relocating them to America, where they settled in Washington Heights, NY. My family was so grateful to live in America and loved it as their own. Several years later, I was born, the only family member born in the United States. Not knowing the language and following Greek tradition, all my parents cared about was my baptismal name, Fotini. They left the legal name to my 10-year-old cousin/*nouna* (godmother) who decided to name me Fiffy Linda, made official on my birth certificate. I was the bridge between their old and new worlds.

In New York, my family built a community, surrounded by loving family and new friends from the St. Spyridon Greek Orthodox Church. We were living the true American Dream, where dad worked seven days a week, and my mother was dedicated to keeping a clean home and keeping our bellies full. We lived in an apartment complex with my first cousins, who were raised like siblings. My brother, my cousins, and I had a great childhood, living for the first ten years of my life across the street from church. Our lives centered around the church both spiritually as we attended church regularly, as well as socially, as we would spend much time outside of church with those we met while in attendance. I remember fondly spending our summers with both my church family and my actual family in a share house at Rockaway Beach. I can remember those summers so vividly, where we would spend our days basking in the sun, skin burnt but big smiles, and then reconvene in our communal kitchen where we would share so many laughs.

After countless years of hard work and assimilating to the United States, my parents were so proud of their kids and their spouses, as they realized they truly accomplished the American Dream, leaving the struggles they left behind to build a beautiful life in perpetuity. Our lives were simple but full. Once dad was taken from us, mom was heartbroken and was subsequently diagnosed with cancer, passing ten years later.

Living on Long Island, I raised my children at Archangel Michael Church in Port Washington, NY, but it was not like my childhood. I was always a member of the church, but for many years, it's almost as if I lost my foundation, my footing, and my connection to my faith. Years later, I had a falling out with some friends whose lives were centered on drama and materialistic wants and desires. I did a lot of soul searching, which led me back to church where I reconnected with my faith, committed to being more involved and to making friends with common interest and kind hearts. I was so blessed to meet women from different socioeconomic backgrounds but with a shared commitment to their faith and who focus on loving fully, and not on driving the most expensive cars. It was then that I joined Bible Study, got more involved in the Philoptochos (the philanthropic ministry of the church), and I was nominated to be a Parish council member. Through these new experiences, I have reconnected with my past and reignited the legacy my parents worked so hard to build for our family. Hard work and love for their family were what mattered to them, and they instilled in me to love unconditionally and to forgive as what is often taught in church.

Thanks to my parents, I have never faltered to love fiercely and unconditionally, and to commit my life to creating a safe and loving environment in which my children can flourish. Today, I have two adult daughters with my husband, one of whom has special needs, and my wish is that they both carry our legacy and our love for our faith as they navigate the highs and lows of their lives.

Noreen Williams

Noreen Williams is a first-generation American whose parents were Irish immigrants. Noreen was raised in Queens and attended Catholic school. She graduated from Queens College and was accepted into the management trainee program at a local community bank, working her way up to assistant vice president in the Commercial Lending Department. She met her husband, Tommy, at a local Irish pub, and they have been married for 25 years.

When her first son was born in 2000, she became a stay-at-home mother. Noreen and Tommy would add another son three years later and finish their family with a daughter four years after that. Noreen developed an interest in Clinical Social Work and enrolled in Fordham University to pursue her graduate degree in social work. She managed to finish the last semester and attend graduation while going through chemotherapy treatment after the diagnosis of breast cancer. She was able to get her dream job, and now she works in a middle school. Noreen realizes how fortunate she is to have her health, to love her job, and to be blessed to have a strong marriage with three kids who mean the world to her.

The author and her mother, Bridget

EXCERPT

My mother, Bridget, came to this country, from Ireland, at the age of 16 years, without her family. She came to live with an aunt and cousins that she did not know at all. She was a very practical person. Coming from Ireland at 16 years of age and her practicality are two aspects of her life that greatly influenced how she raised her kids, especially through the teenage years. These two factors were also brought to my attention constantly growing up.

Practicality

[Irish]

Noreen Williams

My mother, Bridget, came to this country, from Ireland, at the age of 16 years, without her family. She came to live with an aunt and cousins that she did not know at all. She was a very practical person. Coming from Ireland at 16 years of age and her practicality are two aspects of her life that greatly influenced how she raised her kids, especially through the teenage years. These two factors were also brought to my attention constantly growing up.

In America, teenage years are known for excessive wants, self-involved behavior, striving to keep up with peers, and rebelling against your parents. At no point did I believe my mother understood any of these American characteristics. The young girl from Ireland, who came to New York to find a better life for herself would get very irritated at the frivolous nature of being a teenager in the American culture. It created many struggles within our relationship that I would not begin to understand until I would raise my own teenagers. During the neon, over-the-top 1980s, all I knew was that she did not understand me, and this created some resentment within our relationship.

I remember wanting to go to a Shaun Cassidy concert at about 13 years of age, and I wanted to buy every album that came out. My mother would laugh at the silliness of worshipping celebrities. She allowed me to have a few posters on my wall but thought it was ridiculous to spend money on fan devotion. I was being raised by a woman who would tell a story often that I could not even comprehend. When my mother first came to the country at the age of 16 years, she went to work in Manhattan. I was always amazed at how much independence she had at such an early age.

One day, on her way home from work, she saw a huge crowd of people cheering and yelling. A bunch of girls about her age had surrounded a bus. Right away, she thought that something must be wrong and could not imagine why these girls would act like this. Further down the block, she asked what was going on. Someone told her that it was the Beatles. John, Paul, Ringo, and George were right inside that bus with fans screaming outside!!! My mother continued to walk on. When I asked why she did not stay and try to see them, she calmly told me that she had to get home. It made no sense to her to try and get a glimpse of them. For what reason? She thought those girls were crazy. We would never see eye to eye on this subject. I would save money to buy *Tiger Beat* magazines so that I could stare at my favorite stars and learn more about their lives. My mother thought supporting such nonsense was a waste of money.

Keeping up with your peers through the latest clothing trends is pretty important when you are an American teenager. My mother was never going to go for that! At a very young age, I remember fighting over wanting to wear knee socks and not short bobby socks. My mother believed in buying top name brand clothing that would last, but not trendy clothes from popular boutiques. This became a big issue when it came to purchasing a prom dress! At first, she tried to make one on her own, not an impossible endeavor because she had made clothes before and even dresses for a wedding party. But bridesmaid dresses for a wedding in the 1970s was a simpler design than a prom dress in the 1980s! Trying to sew the dress went on for a few weeks but never fully came together. We did not shop for a dress together, as many of my friends did. Then a beautiful, cream-colored, lace dress appeared in my room one day. It was in style, and I loved it!

My parents did not pay for any of the things that came with attending the prom. I had to earn and pay for the expensive ticket, limo, and night out after the prom. I was lucky that it was not uncommon to do your own hair and makeup. I worked and saved my money. I went and had a great night. I never saw the dress again and am pretty confident that my mother returned the dress after the prom. She would never admit to that. However, saving a dress that you spent a lot of money on only to wear it once would really irritate her. This was the closest she came to giving in to American teenage extravagance, and I look back with both gratitude and some embarrassment.

With time, I learned that begging and crying were not the way to my mother's heart. I had to ask for certain items for holidays or birthdays, knowing that maybe one might show up. I really had to wait until I started working to make my own money to spend it on things that she would not buy for me. I was fortunate that even though she thought so many of the things that I felt I had to have were a complete waste of money, she did not forbid me to purchase things on my own. It was hard to always believe that my mother thought things that mattered to me were a waste of time and money. She had a very difficult time seeing things from my perspective.

I realized years later how difficult it must have been to relate to me as a teenager. She came to this country at 16 and had to support herself. She did not have extra money to purchase needless items. American culture seemed more wasteful than the Irish culture. There was a lot to adjust to for a woman trying to raise her children in a time known for extravagance and over-the-top materialism.

My mother brought another interesting aspect to parenting teenagers in America. She believed that you were mature enough to handle a lot at a younger age than many of her peers. I often heard her say that she had come to this country at 16 and had to make it on her own. I did not have a curfew, and I had to figure out how to get to and from places on my own. Now, I am always available to drive my kids anywhere because I hate depending on others.

My parents gave me a good sense of family, but the definitions were probably a little different based on both my upbringing in New York and my mother growing up and leaving Ireland at a young age. I expect my children to eat dinner with us and change their schedules to make time together as a family. Growing up, my family lived separate lives and got together when we could. My mother taught me to count on myself and to make my own decisions confidently. She was not a smothering presence at all. She expected you to be able to handle your life on your own. My mother had to rely on herself and trusted us to do the same. At the time, I resented this and did not believe that she cared enough to be involved. I now realize that my mother put a tremendous amount of trust in me because she felt that I could handle it. She loved me enough to let me figure it out on my own.

My mother did not get the chance to watch her children parent their own kids. Sadly, she died at the young age of 53 years from cancer. Considering how short her life would end up being, she really was an adult at a young age. Things that I did not understand at the time, such as her practical nature, I now realize contributed to my being able to stand on my own. I now have the perspective to see that she was wise not to succumb to superficial wants; on the other hand, I also recognize the necessity of giving in occasionally to items that seem frivolous but bring joy to our lives.

Ashley Tavormina

Ashley Tavormina is a 35-year-old mother to an adorable boy named Russell. Ashley is on track to graduate from Molloy University in May 2023, which has been a lifelong dream. Family is a core motivator for her. Pursuing her dreams and creating a better life for her family is her driving force. Witnessing stereotypes her mother has faced due to her work environment and struggles to support her and her sister kept Ashley motivated to continue working toward finishing her education. She is grateful for the challenges in her past, as they made Ashley who she is today. Her mother, Glenda never once gave up, no matter how challenging. Her mother always worked through difficult times, and as an immigrant pushed through the judgement of others. Ashley hopes to have a long career in the field of education. She also hopes to pay it forward to the great teachers she had in school and to her most significant teacher of all, her mother, the true definition of strength and perseverance, who deserves all the accolades.

The author with her mom, Glenda

EXCERPT

Every year for as long as I was old enough to drive and had my own money, I would go to whichever deli my mother worked to give her flowers for her birthday. And each year, I would shock the people she worked with because I looked nothing like my mother.

Ode to Glendita

[Honduran]

Ashley Tavormina

"Who are those flowers for?" the man behind the counter asked, looking at me with a bouquet in my hand. "They are for my mom," I replied, already knowing he had no idea to whom I was referring. I am used to no one putting together who my mom is just by looking at me. "Who is your mom?" he says, puzzled. "Glenda. Today is her birthday." The man, still trying to make the connection, calls my mother over to receive her flowers.

Every year for as long as I was old enough to drive and had my own money, I would go to whichever deli my mother worked to give her flowers for her birthday. And each year, I would shock the people she worked with because I looked nothing like my mother.

My beautiful mother has dark curly hair, smooth olive skin, dark eyes and is about 5 ft 1 in. I received more of my father's genes as he was a tall Irish man. When asked about my nationality, I am always proud to express how my mother is from Honduras and arrived in this country when she was 10 years old, and my father's family is of Irish descent. I still tease my mother because as much as I embrace my Honduran background, I don't resemble her at all, and she did not teach us (my sister and me) Spanish. "Ashley, your father, didn't understand Spanish; I didn't want to teach you and have him be left out." My sister and I still tease her about this to this day. My father passed away in 2000, but one thing to note about him, he loved everything about my mother, especially her nationality and her many family traditions. I don't think he would have minded at all if we all learned Spanish. Fast-forward to today, and she is teaching my son Spanish, which I am thrilled about.

Growing up without my father, my mother had to take on multiple roles, and I developed much of my work ethic by learning from her. She worked at the deli after my father passed, not because she lacked skills, but because it provided hours necessary for a single mother during that period. In addition, I have fond memories of my mother creating and writing lessons for me after school to help with my phonics and writing. She has a natural teaching instinct and ability, and an incredible sense of detail. "You are too stiff, honey. Here, follow me," my mother would say and then teach me to dance as "Vivir Mi Vida" played in the kitchen. The more I dive into my own reasoning to be an educator, the more I realize my mom subconsciously inspired my love for teaching by having her teach me.

It took me a long time to realize that families from both mothers' and fathers' sides did not always celebrate holidays together. My mother is one of five sisters, all who came to America at different times when they were just young girls, and for as long as I can remember, we have been together for the holidays, no matter the space. My Abuela is the matriarch in the family, and we respect and ensure she is always taken care of and gather all together. I was lucky because my dad's side (Irish) always came over, too, for the holidays. So, for Thanksgiving, there would be turkey, gravy, and cornbread, but it was completely normal to me that rice and beans, platanos, and sometimes homemade tamales were also at our table. It was all I knew. When I see my mom with all my Tías together, there is a sense of love I am grateful for even to this day.

When thinking about my life and my relationship with my mother, there are several instances when she told me about unfortunate stereotypical situations that occurred. Hearing stories like this now, being a mother myself, I think how hard it must have been for her. "They thought I was the nanny," my mother expressed one afternoon. "They thought your aunt Tracey was your mother, and I was just the nanny, but don't worry, I made sure they understood you were mine." She expressed proudly.

I didn't always share moments like this with my mother, but I would get deeply defensive if anyone ever questioned her or tried to make her feel anything less than the amazing person she is. My mother worked in the service industry most of my life, and in that line of business, people pass judgment and can be mean. I tried my best to make sure she always felt special no matter our circumstances. Even as I got older and my closest friends and I would have mother–daughter nights, I wanted to ensure she always felt special. This is no way to say she felt anything less than perfect, but as her daughter and with some of the unfortunate cards we were dealt, it was critical to me to make sure she felt important.

"Honey, I'll get Russell again tomorrow. You go to the library to finish your schoolwork," she says while we look at our table calendars together. I am the first one in my immediate family on the path to graduate from college, and my mother, during this process, has been instrumental. At this point in her life, she has been able to retire, enjoy and be there for her family in ways she was unable to many years ago. "Adios, Grandma!" Russell exclaims, following my mother to the door. Hearing my mom speak Spanish to my son is a full-circle moment. It reminds me that no matter how different she and I might look, there is not a day that goes by that I don't feel internally grateful that this strong woman, who has inspired and taught me in more ways than one, is my mother. She will always get flowers from me.

Mubina Khan Schroeder

Mubina Khan Schroeder is a born-and-raised New Yorker who is the child of immigrants from India and Pakistan. She spent her childhood exploring the streets and wonders of New York City with her mother, Shahjahan Banu Khan, as her closest companion. Her mother also taught in New York City public schools and her father, Shujaat Ali Khan, was a professor of economics at the City University of New York. She credits her parents with her love of learning science and for always exploring. She is currently an associate professor in the School of Education and Human Services at Molloy University. Dr. Schroeder teaches graduate and doctoral-level courses in cognitive sciences, science pedagogy, and neurodiversity.

The author and a picture of her mother, Shahjahan Banu Khan

EXCERPT

Do you know about quantum entanglement? It's when paired particles are linked, no matter how much distance is between them. In the past few years, I have been reading about it obsessively—not because I harbor a natural curiosity about quantum mechanics—but because I love my mom so fiercely and want so badly to believe that her particles and mine will be forever connected, regardless of space and time.

Better Than a Thousand Sons

[Indian; Pakistani]

Mubina Khan Schroeder

I was my mom's only child and sometimes, I'd ask her if she wished I was a boy because I knew in the tradition of her Indian/Pakistani culture that having a male child was considered better for a family. She would always reply with the same response: that I was better than a thousand sons. I lost my mom too early, although I suppose losing one's mom always feels like it's too early.

Every year, as the anniversary of my mom's death approaches, the pain of losing her to such a brutal illness becomes acute and feels as fresh as though her death was yesterday. I've come to the realization that I will never stop missing her and that my longing for her is my love for her prevailing.

When she passed away after a protracted illness, I was both prepared and unprepared to lose her. Here is what I wrote about my mom as I sat in the hospital, next to her, after she passed away:

Do you know about quantum entanglement? It's when paired particles are linked, no matter how much distance is between them. In the past few years, I have been reading about it obsessively—not because I harbor a natural curiosity about quantum mechanics—but because I love my mom so fiercely and want so badly to believe that her particles and mine will be forever connected, regardless of space and time.

I can't find words to really capture the eloquence of her person. She really was that incredible—but I'll try and relate some glimpses of my mom, Shahjahan Banu Khan:

Mom was born in Delhi, India. Girls in her family typically did not go to school, so she taught herself how to read and forced my Nana (grandfather) to enroll her in school at grade six. At some point in her childhood, she also decided she didn't like her given name, Banu, so she replaced it with Shahjahan, which means King of the Realm, and is the name of the Mughal king who built the Taj Mahal, a story, I was told, she avidly read repeatedly as a child. It has been her name ever since.

Before settling for good in New York City, mom lived in India, Pakistan, and different countries in Africa. She had the opportunity to travel widely, and she took me on many trips to Europe, to the Middle East, to her homeland and on numerous pilgrimages. Her faith in the Divine was always unwavering, and when I would express skepticism, she'd tell me, "Don't be so arrogant as to think we humans truly understand the nature of reality."

My mom loved living in New York City: "It's the city that never sleeps!" she would often tell me. Although she told me she was a little scared when she first arrived here in the 1970s, she said she loved exploring and finding new things in the city. It was a common for her to strike up conversations with strangers and she made friends from all over the city, and subsequently, the world.

Someone mentioned to me that mom was so easy to make happy—and it's very true. She was the kind of person who was excited about everyday things. She had a habit of waking me up at dawn during the summer (something I was not pleased about since I will never be a morning person). "Listen to the birds saluting the world!" she would marvel. Among her many qualities, this might be what I loved the most: that she was always so enthusiastic about everything. I never saw anyone so thrilled about something as simple as blades of grass peeking through cracks in the sidewalk or an especially delicious samosa or the brilliant colors of a humble petunia—the vividness of these memories with her both empower me and haunt me.

Despite her enthusiasm and positivity, my mom experienced way too many heartbreaks in her life. Life was incredibly, unrelentingly cruel to her at so many moments: witnessing her endless hardships was hard on me and created some very dark corners in my mind, but she herself never succumbed to bitterness. Somehow, despite it all, she retained a good sense of humor and an eternal hopefulness for better days. My mom used her disarming smile and contagious laugh with abandon. She adored cheesy 1980s movies and would try (and fail) at retelling the goofy jokes from the scripts. She made an amazing chicken pulao biryani, and one of my favorite memories was a wintery December day watching an all-day movie marathon of her making: *What About Bob? The 'Burbs*, and *Pakeezah*, (three of her favorites and, yes, in that order) filling up on biryani and drinking endless cups of her chai.

My mom was an enthusiastic gardener, and she had a habit of leaving one or two containers of weeds growing in them. "Everything deserves a chance. I didn't have the heart to pull these weeds that were trying to survive," she told me. It is for this reason that she was loved by her students: She taught at Forest Hills High School, Aviation High School, and then, finally, Sheepshead Bay High School. She wasn't just my biggest supporter, but she was everyone's champion. Students would still call or e-mail her after they graduated, seeking advice or just staying in touch. Two of her former students from over 15 years ago lived in my parents' neighborhood—when they heard about mom's funeral, they both came and helped carry her to the burial site.

Soon after she retired, mom started experiencing unexplained falls. She was finally diagnosed with a devastating motor-deterioration condition called progressive supranuclear palsy, an illness that is as ugly as it sounds. Her mind mostly stayed intact as she lost control of her muscles over the course of a few years. She effectively became a prisoner in her own body. It was heartbreaking to witness and, when she couldn't communicate, people often incorrectly assumed she had Alzheimer's, which must have made her so sad. She fought fiercely to get better, but in the end, it was too much. She was 72 years old.

Since mom was ill for a long time, I thought I would be prepared. But when the time came, I was not ready to have her leave. Our family had gathered in the hospital to discuss her medical care. We were in anguish because the hospital was encouraging us to pull her ventilator (she had a bad bout of pneumonia), but she appeared to be getting better. As her health care proxy, the decision weighed incredibly heavily on me, and I didn't want to take her off the ventilator. So, as she always did, she decided to do things on her own terms and not trouble anyone—She chose to go when she was surrounded by her loved ones. Her heart simply stopped on its own in the evening and she could not be revived.

I am among the first in my friends to lose her mother. And losing her has changed me forever—just like I can't articulate my mom's incredible personality in words, I am unable to describe the vastness of her absence. My most ancient and deepest fear—not having my mother—has finally been realized and it is even more awful than I had anticipated. What you don't realize is that when someone you love that much dies, a version of you dies with them. Despite this, her death was profoundly graceful, and it brought our splintered family together. We all spent time with her after she passed away, family members who hadn't spoken together in months helped each other as we bathed and prepared her body, we prayed for her, and we buried her in the same cemetery as where my son, Zacherieh, is resting. My mom's face was more peaceful than it has been in months. I like to think she's finally free after all the struggle and that she will be taking care of Zach for me, all our particles forever in harmony with one another.

If you're reading this, stop and call your mom; or better yet, go and spend time with her. Plan a trip, or two, or three with her while she can walk and talk. Ask her about her childhood. Write down her recipes. Record her voice. Forgive each other. Because one day, she'll be gone, and you'll walk into her home, and you'll see signs of her, but she won't be there. You'll be reduced to sobbing over her handwriting, or over old voicemails, or burying your face into her pillow so that you can smell her again. The world as you know it will be changed forever—you'll be motherless. Because there is no one in the world like your mother.

Nadia Khan-Roopnarine

Nadia Khan-Roopnarine, EdD, is the daughter of Nadira Khan and Azad Khan. Nadia's parents are Indo-Caribbean immigrants from Guyana. Though Nadia's parents immigrated to the United States of America as teenagers, the upbringing she and her three siblings received was very traditionally Guyanese. While Nadia cannot quite capture the cadence of her mother's Indo-Guyanese Creole in her own speech, she joyfully works on her accent with her husband, who is also a child of Indo-Guyanese immigrants. Nadia is currently an assistant professor of adolescent English education at St. Joseph's University in New York.

The author's mom, Nadira Khan

EXCERPT

Twice migrated, first from colonized India to indentureship in Guyana/Trinidad, then to America/Canada, Indo-Caribbean women are full of vibrant phrases and specific superstitions that have endured over time and place. [...] As I prepare to be a mother myself to a second-generation American, I find myself clinging to these phrases. I joke with my parents that I would like them to speak with heavy accents to my soon-to-be-born child so that my child can be connected to our Guyanese roots. But through me, I know they will be. These phrases are one of our few remaining links to the generations of women before us, and, as my mom did, I will make sure they endure.

Guidance from a Guyanese Mother

[Guyanese]

Nadia Khan-Roopnarine

Twice migrated, first from colonized India to indentureship in Guyana/Trinidad, then to America/Canada, Indo-Caribbean women are full of vibrant phrases and specific superstitions that have endured over time and place. The phrases captured here have traveled on the tongues of Indian women for generations. Though they don't represent all the sage wisdom one can receive from these women, I recollect here some examples of admonitions and advice my own Guyanese mother, Nadira Khan, has passed to me.

1. For Healthy Interpersonal Relationships:
(a) "Nah tek sharp object or peppa from somebody hand, aya two guh fight" (If you pass peppers of any sort or any sharp objects like knives or scissors from one person's hand to another, it will surely start an argument between the two people).

I have been unfortunate enough to pass a scissor to my brother in front of my mother, who immediately began chastising me and telling my brother to hand it back to me. Apparently, this reverses the potential for a fight. However, it did lead to an argument between myself and my mother, as I was a surly teenager who resented being scolded for something that appeared trivial to me. Since then, though, I have not passed a knife, scissor, pepper, or similar object directly to someone.

(b) "Nah gee shoes fa ppl yuh wan keep in yuh life" (Don't buy or give a person shoes as a gift, because they will walk out of your life.)

Fortunately, this saying has a loophole. If someone buys you shoes or gives them to you as a gift, you can "pay" them for the shoes, thereby canceling out the gift nature of the shoes. Thus, in my family, when someone receives a new pair of slippers, sneakers, stilettos, boots, or the like, it is common to see the passing of a dollar from the gift recipient to the gifter. Needless to say, my mom has an extensive shoe collection and a regular supply of dollar bills on hand.

2. On Faith:
"God nah come, but eyuh send" (God doesn't come to help you with your problems, but God provides what you need in order to navigate them on your own.)

This is a common remark from my mom when she gets a prime parking spot at the grocery store or mall. While I don't think finding parking close to a store door is what this phrase is meant to capture, it's one that helps me through small inconveniences and major challenges. It's always good to have a reminder that I am capable of making my way through problems.

3. **On Mental Health:**
"Bird guh make nest with yuh trow way hair and yuh guh go mad" (In other words, don't throw away your fallen or cut hair outside. Otherwise, birds will use it to make their nests which will cause you to go mad.)

I vividly remember my grandmother sticking to this rule and using her fallen hair to create her own hair ties. In addition to journaling and regular mental health check-ins with professional providers, I always gather my frequently fallen hairs and wrap them tightly before throwing them away. Sorry, birds.

4. **My Mother's Words on Marriage:**
(a) "Nah eat from pot. Ee gah rain on yuh wedding day" (If you take food directly out of the pot and eat it, it will rain on your wedding day.)

I can say with certainty that I frequently stole choice pieces of beef out of the curry pot when my mom was cooking. My wedding day was a beautiful summer day, with light breeze, and not a drop of precipitation. Will I repeat this phrase to my own children to prevent them from sticking their hands in pots of food I've cooked? Absolutely.

(b) "Nah mek broom sweep yuh feet, yuh na guh married" (If a broom passes over your feet, you will never get married.)

I have no recollection of a broom ever passing over my feet, and I am happily married. Do we call this proof? Perhaps.

5. **How to Avoid Encounters with Unwanted Supernatural Entities:**
(a) "Tie up yuh hair or churile ga get yuh" (A churile, a vehemently hostile female spirit created after a woman dies in childbirth, lurks to grab ahold of unsuspecting women by the hair, if they do not tie it up.)

Something in this superstition feels akin to control of the female body to me. Indo-Caribbean women have notoriously long and thick hair. Does this superstition exist to prevent us from "flaunting" this asset? Either way, I always tie my hair with a scrunchie, regardless of length, before getting out of my car at night. Why risk it?

(b) "Must always walk inna house backward when yuh come in at night" (Walking in with your back to the door is the surest way to shake off the jumbies [bad spirits] that will attempt to enter your home with you.).

Why are they only present at night? Is this superstition rooted in the habit of looking behind you for intruders before you go into the house? All I know is, I've never entered the house facing forward after midnight.

6. **On Developing a Good Relationship with Money:**
(a) "Yuh nah respect money if yuh purse deh on de ground" (If you put your purse or wallet on the ground, it means you do not have respect for money and wealth.).

Now, for more practical reasons, I never let my purse or wallet touch the ground. I make sure it's in eyesight or on my body, mostly because I don't want my items stolen. Depending on where I am, I also avoid placing my bags on the ground for fear of bugs and other critters crawling in. But I will say, I have never been without money I needed.

And a particular favorite of mine, especially when I was a teenager tasked with chores…

(b) "If yuh sweep past 6 aclock in the afternoon yuh sweep way yuh wealth" (Sweeping dust out the door is akin to sweeping away money and wealth.).

Dust was swept out of the door in Guyana, not into a dustpan and garbage can. Thus, the superstition involves sweeping things out of your home. As a wily teen, I exploited the ambiguity of the phrase, so I often saved sweeping the kitchen floor for last on my list of chores because it was usually dark by the time I got to it. I would make a big show of not being able to do it because the sun had already set.

7. **And Ultimately, on Learning:**
"If yuh cyan hear, yuh mus feel" (If you do not listen to someone's advice or rules, you will face the consequences of your choice.).

While this may not seem like a menacing phrase, it was usually being stated after I disobeyed a rule or direction. For example, if I was told not to climb on some rocks at the beach and proceeded to do so anyway, this is the phrase I would have heard. The effect would be immediate, and I would swiftly climb down from the rocks for fear of a physical consequence.

As I prepare to be a mother myself to a second-generation American, I find myself clinging to these phrases. I joke with my parents that I would like them to speak with heavy accents to my soon-to-be-born child so that my child can be connected to our Guyanese roots. But through me, I know they will be. These phrases are one of our few remaining links to the generations of women before us, and, as my mom did, I will make sure they endure.

Sherone Smith-Sánchez, EdD, is the proud mother of Manuel J. Ortiz (age 38 years), Orael M. Sanchez (age 29 years), Sehra I. Sanchez (age 23 years), and Josiah E. Sanchez (age 18 years). She is also the wife of Eduardo L. Sanchez. Sherone migrated to the United States at 20 years old, from the island of Jamaica. She is a member of clergy, professor, and president of Talawah Turf International. Her most recent book, *Talawah Turf*, was published in 2013, and *Sabbath of the Mind* will be published in 2023. Her passion lies in loving fellow humans and supporting their journeys to wholeness and personal and professional advancement.

Manuel J. Ortiz, author, singer, and senior anesthesiology technician is focused on building a kinder generation. Manuel is father to Liam and Noah Ortiz. Manuel's latest children's book *Noah's Lost Building Block* was inspired by his sons and was published in 2021.

Orael M. Sanchez, musician, social media influencer, and mental health professional, considers herself a change-agent for today's society. Orael has worked in the field of mental health and social service for five years. She is a graduate of Queens College, where she earned a baccalaureate in psychology. Orael currently attends Howard University where she is pursuing a master's degree in social work.

Sehra I. Sanchez, visual and performing artist, showcases her work in her own virtual gallery called *Iana's Illustrations* on her Instagram platform. In 2023, Sehra will co-release a children's book titled *Chocolate Brown* as its illustrator. She is also an accomplished liturgical dancer and has represented her school at the Aquinas Conference in Michigan. Sehra is completing studies at Molloy University, where she is pursuing a baccalaureate in visual arts.

Josiah E. Sanchez is a recent graduate of Evangel Christian High School. He is a writer and a freshman pursuing communications in media at Molloy University. Josiah's interests lie in philosophy and in serving his community. As such, he has volunteered with Lutheran Social Services of NY in the Office of Advancement and Communications and has recently served his community via his work with the village of Valley Stream.

EXCERPT

Entering a new and strange country as an immigrant is like suddenly walking out of a bright, peaceful, familiar hall and entering a dark, smelly, huge, and scary room. In fact, my final graduation project in art school, in the United States, was an environmental installation called "Blue Room." It was a small closet-like space lined with old mattresses with varying textured and jagged pieces all around it. Now that I reflect, "Blue Room" was a summary of my initial years as an immigrant art student, building the resiliency needed to survive this experience.

Mother and Children Discuss Immigrant Experiences

[Jamaican]

Sherone Smith-Sánchez and Her Children

Developing an Identity

Dear Momma,

Being the child of an immigrant means I never get to feel like I am one culture or another. I sometimes feel that I'm never enough of any one culture. I once spoke with a woman at church who teased me that I wasn't "truly Jamaican" because I couldn't speak the language. It hurt. It cut deep, not because it was correct but because I was a young woman who was trying to figure out who she was and where she wanted to go. I didn't understand or speak your dialect, Patois, fluently, nor do I understand what happens on the island from a first-person perspective. Due to that, it's hard for me to feel like I am genuinely Jamaican. An example emphasizing my point is when I cook Japanese food, that doesn't make me Japanese. Similarly, I feel that cooking Jamaican food doesn't make me Jamaican. I struggle with being a "genuine" Jamaican, at least in my subconscious.

Truthfully, there are certain traditions in our culture that I have not embraced and some I have. To you, they are traditions that were passed down for years and years. Ideally, as I grow, I will make decisions about the traditions I'll keep and the ones I'll let go. We wear the same size, but still I cannot fit in your shoes.

Visiting Jamaica taught me some of the islander parts of myself. I learned that I love birds and deeply dislike mosquitoes. I dislike mosquitoes as much as they like me! Walking through the island, I fell in love with nature and all the fruit-bearing trees. I gazed at the hazy Blue Mountains and the hummingbirds zipping around and felt a sense of wonder. I learned that I value serenity, quiet, and all the things that are scarce here but are so abundant there.

See you later,
Sehra

Education, Gaming the American Teen Way

Hi Mama,

Here is my memory of a story of an event that could have only happened to the son of an immigrant, focused on us advancing through education:

So as a teen, I really didn't go out much. I wasn't a party teen so to speak. All I can remember doing is working and going to school and, as a getaway from all things going on at the time, playing my video games. PlayStation was my gaming console at the time. Now, this was still in the times where you had to invite or go over each other's houses to play with a friend (no online playing). Well, working a part time job, going to school, and gaming really do not work well in a house where schooling is the most important standard. Because I was playing video games all hours of the night, I was tired and being tired all the time led to my not doing so well in school. You can guess what followed … that's right, no gaming for me! This was DEVASTATING to my daily routine after school and work. So I decided to grab my PlayStation and hook it up to the only TV that worked in my sister Orael's room. And I got away with this for about a week. Until, for whatever reason, I did the whole 007 routine, started playing and went all the way downstairs to my room without bringing my PlayStation.

That ill-fated day was a Friday, and on Saturdays, I would normally sleep in. But not this Saturday. I was awakened by the door to the top steps being flung open and the slow motion of my PlayStation in midair as I tried to run to catch it like a parent trying to catch a baby before the baby falls off the couch. Needless to say, I was not fast enough. My PlayStation hit the back wall along with the controllers, and the disk flew out and got all scratched up. As I looked up at the top of the stairs, my mom was there looking down with a grin. "Son, I told you no games until you get your grades up." I learned three things that day: (1) Mom really didn't like video games; (2) She was waiting for a reason to throw that PlayStation against the wall; and (3) Drink coffee.

All in all, I paved the road for my siblings to enjoy gaming in a more relaxed house environment and a good balance between school and gaming that I didn't have. So Orael, Sehra, and Josiah, I love you and you're welcome. Oh, and RIP PlayStation 1.

Love,
Manny

Weird Experiences

Dear Mom,

You asked me what "weird experiences" I've had as the child of a Jamaican immigrant. Honestly, most of the experiences are "weird." Being a second-generation Jamaican immigrant means that I've been asked stupid questions like: "Do you smoke weed?" and "Does your mom wash her locs?" (Locs are small traditional hair rolls, commemorative of a Nazarene Covenant). Being a second-generation immigrant means that I've heard angry remarks about how I should "go back to my country" as if (a) I wasn't born here and (b) Going to my mother's childhood home on my beautiful island would be a punishment.

Being the daughter of an immigrant means other immigrants will attempt to devalue my "Jamaican-ness" while those born on American soil will tell me I am too "ethnic." It means, they'll tell me to pick between a burger and jerk pork. It means I've become resilient, *talawah*, as you say. I know myself. I love myself. I love where you, and therefore I, come from. So, what's "weird" to me is that others fail to see the beauty in this, and that they'll never know how good a burger and jerk pork taste in the same plate.

Love,
Your Jama-rican daughter, Orael

Interesting Cultural Differences

Hello Mom,

My story about having an immigrant parent began when we were talking one day. I don't recall how we ended up on the topic, but we were talking about dogs. Specifically, you told me that in the island of Jamaica where you were born, most dogs were outside dogs. Not only this but that dogs from several homes would walk together through the towns and even get food together.

I have seen stray cats and dogs here in the United States, but never ones in groups or with homes to go back to. I had forgotten you had told me that and was pleasantly surprised upon visiting the island for myself. I found it interesting. I noticed an interesting cultural difference then. Sometimes it's hard to differentiate between what's your culture and just your personality.

Love,
Josiah

With Love, from Your Jamaican Mama

My Dear Children,

Entering a new and strange country as an immigrant is like suddenly walking out of a bright, peaceful, familiar hall and entering a dark, smelly, huge, and scary room. In fact, my final graduation project in art school, in the United States, was an environmental installation called "Blue Room." It was a small closet-like space lined with old mattresses with varying textured and jagged pieces all around it. Now that I reflect, "Blue Room" was a summary of my initial years as an immigrant art student, building the resiliency needed to survive this experience.

Back then, as I groped around in the dark, weeping daily, I had only the memories of my homeland mixed with hope for the future to guide me. But in this strange place those memories and traditions did not always serve me well. I kept bumping into things and people who called me "exotic," the "N-word," or because I spoke British English I spoke since infancy, "uppity." Once some befriended me, they wanted to know why I did not fulfill their stereotypical expectations of a Jamaican and did I "have any weed." For the record, I did not. Still, what I had were the memories, traditions, and behavioral patterns brought with me. They were a part of my identity, and the only tools I had. So, I made a conscious decision to navigate the traumatic immigrant experience by celebrating them, using them, and gaining more knowledge about my surroundings and the world to share them with you when you finally entered my world through birth and adoption.

Your entries into this world and into my heart turned on a huge light. My aim was to help you to find your own path, not necessarily the life I stumbled through as an immigrant. I must confess that I have experienced such sadness and anger watching them! But … I also love watching your resilience as you deal with each one with grace; and most importantly, I love you!

As usual, I cried as I read your letters, especially seeing the evidence of your self-love. My hope is that you will all live as students of the world, embracing interests, paths, and traditions that fill you all with contentment. Manny, I see that you now understand that the standard of acquiring an education is about gaining access to the billions of 'light switches' throughout the world. Knowledge is power. We wanted you to walk in power. This value is not alien to the recent immigrant (pun intended). The great Stacey Abrams calls this power, "The Trinity of Success." This trinity—having a consistent prayer life, getting a good education, and taking care of one another—involves authentic connections with your God, your family, and deepened knowledge about yourselves and the world that can lead to financial, personal, and spiritual freedom.

It is true that as you all grew, I grew and learned better ways of gifting knowledge to you and to others. I am not sure if I became a better parent as the years rolled on. (Sorry about that PlayStation and the zillions of mistakes made along the way!) I am sure, though, that I am now happy in my immigrant skin as I learn new ways of seeing what is still a strange but not-so-new world.

Love,
Mama
(Sherone Smith-Sánchez)

Life Lessons Learned from Immigrant Grandparents

Opposites Attract   107
　　[Irish; Croatian]
　　Joanne O'Brien

My Immigrant Grandparents   111
　　[Mixed-European]
　　Rickey Moroney

Greek Women in the Family   114
　　[Greek]
　　Peggy Pyrovolakis

Yiayia   118
　　[Greek]
　　Matina Stergiopoulos

The Immigrant Hustle   122
　　[Italian]
　　Tim Roda

My Grandfather, the Legend   126
　　[Greek] [Student Essay]
　　Emanuel Giouroukakis

Growing Up with a Pappou   129
　　(Greek) [Student Essay]
　　Paul Giouroukakis

Joanne O'Brien

Joanne O'Brien earned her BA and MA degrees in English from Fordham University, an MEd in religious education from Boston College, and an EdD in the areas of curriculum and teaching from Teachers College, Columbia University. Joanne's dissertation topic was truancy prevention for children between the ages of 5 and 12 years. Joanne has taught on the elementary, high school, undergraduate, and graduate levels. She has also been a high school chairperson, assistant principal, principal, and associate superintendent. Presently, Joanne is dean of the School of Education and Human Services at Molloy College. Joanne's work has centered on educational advocacy for underserved populations and creating community-based school programs incorporating social work and effective instructional practices. In addition to all of this, she bakes great *pogachas*.

Mary and Joe Kirincic with three of their grandchildren, (from left to right) Joanne O'Brien, John O'Brien, and Virginia Reid

EXCERPT

I attended Teachers College and would drive there from Queens every week and take the West Side Highway South along the Hudson River. While I went on the West Side Highway, I would think about how my grandparents entered this country at the Battery with just their hopes and dreams, and I always said a prayer of thanks for their courage to come to this country and to provide the best they could for their families. I'm grateful to be a beneficiary of that courage and generosity.

The author's paternal Irish grandmother, Mary Cassidy O'Brien, and her children, (left to right) Catherine, Alan, Robert (baby in Mary's arm), and Ellen holding Eileen

Opposites Attract

[Irish; Croatian]

Joanne O'Brien

My father is the son of Irish immigrants, and my mother and her parents are Croatian immigrants. My parents met in the Bronx, were from vastly different households, fell in love, and married. My grandparents were powerful men and women who, in many ways, inspired me to take risks.

Irish Grandmother and Grandfather

My Irish grandmother, Mary Cassidy, came to this country on a ship and went through Ellis Island at the age of 16 years with her brother Tom. Her brother Tom told her that they would reunite in two weeks at a church in Staten Island, and my grandmother was put into service in a household in Manhattan. After two weeks, she went to the Church on Staten Island, but my uncle Tom was not there, and she never saw him again. While numerous relatives searched for what happened to Tom, even going to Ireland on multiple trips, I found his grave in the church cemetery in Drumshanbo, the county seat of Leitrim. He had served in the British Army and had died in 1918.

My grandmother married Henry O'Brien, whom she met on the boat coming to the United States. My grandmother had 12 children. Nine reached adulthood. The first three children were placed into an orphanage because my grandmother had to work, and it was not until they were 6, 7, and 8 years that she could take care of them at home. She subsequently had nine other children. My grandfather was not the most dependable person, so my grandmother was the one who had to manage the household and provide for her children by working as a laundress. I had the good fortune to live next door to my grandmother in the last years of her life, and I vividly remember her telling me stories of Ireland and her childhood there. I would've never known from my grandmother's stories that she was orphaned at a young age and lived in a poor house in Ireland.

When my grandmother and her brother had the chance to come to the United States, they did, and my grandmother never wanted to return to Ireland. She was a very proud citizen of the United States and managed to work and raise her 12 children in different neighborhoods of Manhattan and the Bronx. My grandmother was an eclectic cook and would make pot roast and spaghetti; we were always curious to know how she came up with that combination. She loved to bake. Almost every week in my childhood, I remember her walking over to our house with corn muffins in her apron, and she would flip them out onto our kitchen counter without saying a word and go back to her house next door.

She protected immigrants who were being taken advantage of and there were numerous stories of her stepping in to protect them when they were harassed. I remember the story of her protecting a person on the subway who was being attacked, and she stood up to the attackers and said, "He doesn't know any better. He's a greenhorn!" Another story was when she saw a man whipping his horse, she took the whip from the man and started beating him! She was a stoic woman who never complained about anything.

Croatian Grandfather and Grandmother

My mother's father, Joseph Kirincic, came to the United States in 1912 when he was 16 in search of his future. He lived with his brother Anton and worked with him at Con Edison in Astoria, New York. Realizing a war was coming, he joined the army, where he remained for four years, learned English, did recruiting work with Slavic people, and became a sergeant in France. In 1920, he returned to Krk to see his folks and marry his childhood sweetheart, Mary Brnic. They married and had a daughter Margaret who was my mother. My grandfather returned to New York and settled in Astoria right off Potter Avenue (now 23rd Ave) and 31st St. to establish a home for his wife, young daughter, and, subsequently, three other daughters.

When my grandfather found an apartment and returned to work at Con Edison, he arranged for my grandmother and mother to come to the United States. My grandmother left a small island in the Adriatic with her 2-year-old daughter and traveled north by train to Hamburg, Germany. I have always been in awe of my grandmother for making this trip alone with her 2-year-old daughter. My grandmother, speaking only Croatian, dared to take a 2-year-old through numerous countries and travel across the Atlantic Ocean with her baby to be reunited with her husband in New York.

In my mother's early years, the only language spoken at home was Croatian because it was the only language my grandmother knew. And even though my grandmother lived in this country all her life and died at the age of 86 years, she always spoke a mixture of Croatian and English.

My mother entered school only speaking Croatian, and it was such a traumatic experience for her that when my brother and I were born and my Irish father wanted her to teach us Croatian, she refused to do so. She did not want anything to interfere with our assimilation to school. And while my mother entered school knowing no English, she skipped two grades, went to Hunter High School, and graduated from Hunter College at the age of 20 years with a degree in economics. She married my father four days after her college graduation.

My mother's remembrances to me in her old age were the kindness of her teachers who helped a young immigrant girl assimilate to a new country. When my brother and I were in elementary school, my mother returned to school and earned a master's degree in education from Queens College. She became a teacher, and so did I, as did two of my three aunts.

My grandfather was a very proud citizen of the United States. He memorized the Declaration of Independence and the Gettysburg Address and recited them in perfect English. He insisted that his four daughters go to college, and all of them graduated from Hunter. Meanwhile, my grandmother stayed home, took care of household duties, and raised her daughters.

I fondly remember my grandmother cooking and baking, and happy to be with her family; she needed nothing else. Every holiday, my grandmother made a yeast bread called *pogacha*. I vividly remember my grandmother taking great care to bake this bread and offer it to her family for the holidays. Because it is a yeast bread, my grandmother would carefully place the dough in places in her house that had no drafts and were warm enough to allow the dough to rise.

When she did this baking, throughout the kitchen, there was flour, and pans and towels all over the house, and as she got older, she would forget a step, and some of the dough would not rise, and she would need to throw out the mixture and begin again. I vividly remember my grandmother taking great care to bake these loaves of bread and would be so disappointed when they did not rise. My mother never attempted to bake the bread, and one or two of my aunts tried but gave up because it is a messy process, at least the way we do it. My grandmother did not have a written recipe for *pogacha*, and she made the bread from memory. As her memory failed, so did the baking of *pogachas*.

When my grandmother died in 1983, I asked my mother to call some of her Croatian relatives and ask for their *pogacha* recipes. She received two slightly different ones, so I combined the two recipes. Since my grandmother's death, I have made *pogachas* for all my relatives who like *pogacha* but who never learned how to make it.

Every Christmas, Easter, and Thanksgiving, I make eight *pogachas*. I think of my grandmother every time I bake them and wish we could have baked them with my Kitchen-Aid mixer. The top line of my recipe reads, "First, pray to grandma."

Somewhere in my gene pool, I received the courage of my grandmothers: one of them journeyed from Krk to Germany with a 2-year-old and then crossed the Atlantic. My Irish grandmother came to the United States with her brother, and I'm sure she had no money except the promise of a job to be a laundress in the homes of wealthy New Yorkers. I have always admired my grandmothers and my mother.

I attended Teachers College and would drive there from Queens every week and take the West Side Highway South along the Hudson River. While I went on the West Side Highway, I would think about how my grandparents entered this country at the Battery with just their hopes and dreams, and I always said a prayer of thanks for their courage to come to this country and to provide the best they could for their families. I'm grateful to be a beneficiary of that courage and generosity.

SECTION 5: Life Lessons Learned from Immigrant Grandparents

Rickey Moroney

Rickey Moroney is the granddaughter of immigrants from Europe who met and married here in America, raising their families, living among relatives all their lives in Brooklyn, who never really realized how much they influenced her life until she wrote this essay as an adult. She is grateful for her extended family who surrounded her as she grew up in Brooklyn and then later in Queens. She is an adjunct faculty member at Molloy University in the School of Education and Human Services. She holds a bachelor of fine arts degree from New York Institute of Technology and a master of science degree in education with a concentration in educational technology from Walden University. Rickey currently co-teaches a course for teacher candidates incorporating supervised hands-on experience based on social emotional learning along with children's literature enriching elementary students in a local school.

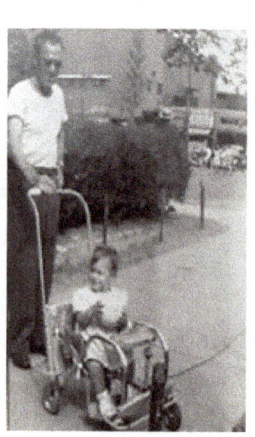

The author with her grandparents (left to right): paternal grandfather Joe, paternal grandmother Anna, maternal grandfather Pobby (Harry), and maternal grandmother Nanny (Edith)

EXCERPT

Besides giving me unconditional love and indulging my every childish whim, they gave me precious memories and helped shape my character as I grew. They laid the foundation for my adulthood by modeling, nurturing, and teaching me so many life lessons. I regret that I didn't ask them more about the life they left behind in their native countries when they journeyed to America.

My Immigrant Grandparents

[Mixed European]

Rickey Moroney

All four of my grandparents were immigrants from various countries in Europe during the early part of the 20th century. I was the first grandchild on both sides of the family. Both my parents were first-born, first-generation Americans.

Besides giving me unconditional love and indulging my every childish whim, they gave me precious memories and helped shape my character as I grew. They laid the foundation for my adulthood by modeling, nurturing, and teaching me so many life lessons. I regret that I didn't ask them more about the life they left behind in their native countries when they journeyed to America.

Grandma Anna (my paternal grandmother) sailed from Germany when she was 16 years of age along with her older sister Dora, who was 18 years of age. Throughout their lives, they remained close, always living together even after they married in two-family homes in the Canarsie section of Brooklyn, NY. My great-aunt Dora was a bonus grandmother to me. My grandmother was a seamstress and worked in the garment district of Manhattan. She and my grandfather, Joe, helped form the International Ladies Garment Workers' Union. My grandmother would sew clothes for me as I grew up, all through high school. I always remember my grandmother in the kitchen, cooking and baking. I would assist her, always observing how she cooked and asking a thousand questions. My grandmother never used a recipe, just knew it by heat. She made wonderfully delicious fruit-filled pastries, delicious soups, and the best hamburger I ever ate. She ground her own chop-meat fresh. I have her meat grinder, which by now is an antique.

I am not sure when my grandpa Joe emigrated from Austria, but I know he fought for America in World War I. He was a tailor, but his real joys came from his pet parakeet, from his small garden behind the row house they lived in where he grew tomatoes, and from making wine in an old bathtub in his basement. I loved playing with his parakeet, helping him weed his garden and pick tomatoes, and watching him make wine. My grandfather bought me a parakeet, who I named Lucky. Unfortunately, Lucky wasn't so lucky. When my mother left the window open in my room one January (she was not an animal lover), I found him lifeless at the bottom of the cage. However, we had plenty of fun and bonding time during his short life.

My grandparents bought me my first two-wheeler for my 7th birthday. When I came to their house, they ushered me into the basement to see my brand-new blue Schwinn two-wheeler, one of the best gifts a 7-year-old could receive. When we stayed over at my grandparents for weekends, we got the run of the house, making elaborate blanket forts and having all the treats we didn't get at home. We would go to the Canarsie shore, Jamaica Bay to take a sightseeing excursion around the bay, watching the scenery, the pleasure boats, and the shorebirds. Then we would sit on the dock and watch the fishermen catch giant eels. As we grew up, my father and grandfather taught my brother and me to play pinochle. Fairly soon, we were beating them at pinochle, maybe because our young minds weren't cluttered and we could remember the cards, or maybe they just let us win.

My maternal grandparents, Harry, a taxicab driver, whose nickname was Rickey (the reason for my name, but we called him Pobby), and Edith (we called her Nanna) were just as special. Pobby came to the United States from England in 1922. He was one of ten children, nine boys and one girl. I had lots of great uncles, always dropping by to visit from time to time. Pobby had an Oldsmobile coupe that he would let me sit in for hours and play with the power windows to my heart's content. We would go for rides, and he taught me how to identify cars by their details. I have retained that skill to this day. I was his faithful companion on his adventures in the neighborhood, Redhook. He took me to the community pool and taught me to swim. He would also take me to the local bar to introduce me to his friends, sit me on a stool, and order two beers—an alcoholic one for him and a root beer for me.

My nanna, Edith, was a bakery saleswoman in a local bakery. She came to the United States as a child from either Germany or Poland (the boarders changed quite frequently during the early 20th century). She had a big scar on her leg from a childhood skating accident, but it never slowed her down. I spent a lot of time with her. We used to go to downtown Brooklyn to the live chicken market to bring home a freshly killed chicken. I remember walking to nanna's house from mine as a very toddler, about two or three buildings away. I thought I was doing it all alone, but my father followed me to make sure I was safe. I remember sitting on her lap at the kitchen window eating apple slices and gouda cheese.

I always had a lot of family around. We all lived in Brooklyn and then some of us moved to Queens. There were always plenty of cousins to play with as well as aunts, uncles, and grandparents to make sure we were safe and happy.

The child I was and the adult I have become have been shaped and influenced by my grandparents; by who they were, what they did for me and with me, and how they cared for and supported me with unconditional love. As a child, I never thought about asking about what their lives were like before they came to America. I wish I had, but I did do some research from the family archives my mother kept and through the Ellis Island Foundation's database. Reflecting on the experiences I had with them has been meaningful, enlightening, joyful, and fulfilling. I appreciate the opportunity to take this trip back in time.

Peggy Pyrovolakis

Born and raised in New Jersey with her two sisters, Peggy is a first-generation Greek-American whose love of her family and of Greece have guided her throughout her life. In the United States, she met a nice Greek boy (every Greek mother's dream), got married, had children, and enrolled her children in a Greek school. She continues the family tradition of vacationing with her kids in Greece every summer. She is married and lives with her husband and two children in NYC. Peggy's father, the youngest of four children, came to America (where his sister and brother had already immigrated) in search of a job from post-WWII Greece, was employed at first as a welder, then a restaurateur. Peggy's mother, the oldest of four children, is the sole person in her family to have left Greece. She left her homeland at the age of 17 years when she married Peggy's father, who had gone back to Greece searching for a good wife for a good life. They got all that and then some.

The author with her mother and grandmother, Panagiota

EXCERPT

It is an honor to share my mother's and my grandmother's ways—not as a historical account, for fear of not capturing it accurately or completely, but instead as a more emotional recollection of a matriarch. The women in a Greek family are the thread that weaves everyone together.

Greek Women in the Family

[Greek]

Peggy Pyrovolakis

If a mother's work is never done, mathematically, then, a grandmother's work would equate to double, or maybe even exponentially, never being done. What about great grandmothers? Could it be infinitely never done? Women, including great grandmothers, grandmothers (Or *yiayias*, as they are endearingly called in Greek), and mothers, are the pillars of Greek-American families. They are the cornerstones of our homes, and the support they give to their loved ones is their tremendous strength, love, and blessings. It is an honor to share *Yiayia* Panagiota's ways—not as a historical account, for fear of not capturing it accurately or completely, but instead as a more emotional recollection of a matriarch. The women in a Greek family are the thread that weaves everyone together.

My mother, the oldest of four, is the only person in her family to have left Greece. She left her homeland at the age of 17 years when she married my father, who had gone back to Greece searching for a good wife for a good life. My grandmother and grandfather hosted him to dinner in their small village, Livadas, in Crete; received my mother's consent; and arranged for them to marry. My parents married in the city of Chania, Crete, and then moved to America. My grandmother adored my father. She spoiled him rotten and would show it by preparing his favorite foods, leaping up from her chair when he walked in the room as a show of respect, and jovially taking his side if my mother was ever complaining. It was quite poignant to watch, as a child. It was evident that she loved my parents, my sisters, and me.

Although it was an arranged marriage, it was truthfully my mother's choice to marry my father. She was quite progressive for her time and wanted to break free from social constraints. Marrying this nice American man gave her the opportunity to start a new life in a new land. My mother's decision, and my grandparents' support, for her to emigrate were rather progressive ideas at the time. Turning away from the ideas of dowry and searching for empowerment demonstrate their quiet strength and fortitude. Unexpectedly, the grief my grandmother felt after her daughter left was insurmountable.

Later, this brave woman, my mother, traveled by herself with her three babies to get back to her homeland Greece and be in her mother's embrace. Year after year, we would go and stay with my grandmother for the entire summer. As we got older, my mother would take us to Greece on the first the day of summer vacation and we would remain there, live there, until the day before school started. We stayed in her village in the mountains of Livadas, Crete, and we stayed in her apartment in the city of Chania.

This was the beginning of my journey to being Greek. It wasn't just visiting Greece with my mother. It was staying in the village that was so different than my home in New Jersey. It was being around my grandmother who soaked up every bit of me when I was there and made me feel like her warmth and attention for three months made up for my absence in the nine months that I wasn't there. She wasn't afraid to show her affection and would hug and kiss me whenever it overcame her. My grandmother would bring rabbits from the pen for us to play with; she would take us through her garden; she would crack almonds with us; she would sing us songs from her childhood; she would share historical accounts of families lost in the war; she would make us *psarosoupa* (fish soup) on the beach while the uncles went fishing. There are so many unique and beautiful memories of things my grandmother would do for us. Because she gave memories, events, time, love, words, advice, and stories, she gave us the things we couldn't buy in our good life back in the States. She exuded love.

When cultures combined on U.S. soil, magic happened! When it came time for my wedding, my entire Greek family came. My uncle, my mother's brother, greeted all our guests with a shot of *tsikoudia* (Cretan moonshine) that he himself made with his grapes and distillery in my grandmother's house in the village. My grandmother came and was treated as a queen. If I weren't the bride, she would have been next in the position of honor—that is the reverence that we gave to her without hesitancy. She deserved it, and she lovingly came to each one of her grandchildren's weddings.

As an adult, I had the greatest pleasure to witness my grandmother dote on my own children. She would put them on her leg and bounce them up and down, singing old Cretan songs to them. Endless supplies of hugs and kisses were brought forth, as were endless homemade treats like *kalitsounia* (savory cheese or spinach pies) and *koulourakia* (butter cookies). She gasped when I told her they didn't want ice cream and was disappointed that she couldn't then run down to the *periptero* (concession stand) to get them some. She paid attention to what they liked and re-created them with her love in her kitchen: homemade cinnamon raisin bread for my son and *Sfakianes pites* (fried cheese fritters, particular to the Sfakia region in Crete) for my daughter (but with peanut butter and cinnamon sugar instead of mizithra cheese).

My grandmother lit up and jumped up when we visited her, no matter how tired or unwell she felt. She would greet us at the door when we arrived and escort us out when we left. While there, she would take me into her kitchen and show me her candle, the religious candle that symbolizes that Christ is in her house. It would remain lit, day and night, protecting those she loves. One of her daily routines was to replenish the oil so that the candle would burn continuously. It would never go out, so the prayers and protection of our Lord would be a constant, without hiccup, without interruption. To me, that candle, which now sits on a shelf in my kitchen, symbolizes a woman's never-ending prayer to her family.

My grandmother would stand at the doorway as we left and would do the sign of the cross in our direction with her prayer, "H panagia mazi sou" (May the Virgin Mary be with you.). This image of her is seared in my brain. Halfway down the stairs, I would turn around and look up to see her doing the sign of the cross on me. Walking down her street, I would look up at her balcony and see her doing the sign of the cross on me from four stories above. It was my shield, coat of armor, protection. Today, I do the same to my children every time they leave the house to go to school or to go out. It is something they know from her, and now from me. It is her legacy.

It would be remiss to not include the grandmother to my children, who carries this love, prayer, and strength another generation down the line. My mother does the same: She waits outside, making the sign of the cross on us in the car, and does not go inside until the car to turns the corner and we are out of sight. No matter how cold, wet, windy it is. She makes her grandkids' favorite foods, no matter how many of them are coming over! And she makes us all feel loved the same way my grandmother did for me.

Being a Greek-American woman, raising children, being on the receiving end of my mother's and grandmother's endless love, strength, and prayers filled me, warmed my bones, soothed my pains, cured my ailments, supported my personal growth, and made me the woman I am today. These Greek grandmothers can rule the world with their strength, love, and prayers—OK, maybe not the entire world, but their worlds—their families. From a mountain village to New York City, these women have shaped my life in an unquantifiable but all-encompassing way and are seared on my soul.

Matina Stergiopoulos

Dr. Matina Barbara Stergiopoulos was raised in Staten Island, Brooklyn, and Queens, New York by her parents, Ellie and Argyris, and her extended family; both her maternal (Georgia and Stratis) and paternal (Matina and Stavros) grandparents. She fondly recalls traveling to Greece every year to spend time at her paternal grandparent's home in Sparta. There she learned to love her language, religion, and culture. Matina's passion for her culture has led to her involvement in Greek organizations, namely, the Archangel Michael Church in Port Washington, New York. Matina is an accomplished school leader with nearly 20 years experience and currently serves as an assistant principal at the Plainview-Old Bethpage Central School District. She earned her EdD in entrepreneurial leadership in education from the Johns Hopkins University in 2020. Matina is the proud mother of Georgios (age 14 years) and Argyrios (age 10 years) and the devoted wife of Dr. Sotirios Stergiopoulos.

The author with (left to right) her grandmother and her mother

EXCERPT

With every turn of her spoon, yiayia offered a lesson. Today's lesson was about being an independent woman. "Leaving the village was not easy. I had a comfortable life. Your grandpappou had made good money as the owner of the kafenio, but, sadly, the Nazis destroyed that. They took all we had, but at least they didn't take our lives. So many suffered. I got away with a lot because I was blonde. I learned then that looks, combined with intelligence, can be a powerful combination."

Yiayia

[Greek]

Matina Stergiopoulos

Honk! Honk! "*Ela!* Come on!" my grandmother yelled. Her right hand held the steering wheel of her baby blue Oldsmobile, while her left hand dangled out of the window, a sleek Kent Golden Lights 100's nestled between her perfectly manicured fingers. She had short, blonde, spikey hair and resembled a Mediterranean Brigitte Nielsen meets Marilyn Monroe. Grandma had movie-star looks, but the scrubs she wore indicated that she was anything but glamorous. Every morning, grandma, or *yiayia* as we called her, woke up at 5 A.M. to work at the local nursing home as a dietician. While the title may sound impressive, her role was simply to serve the residents with food according to their dietary needs. That meant forgoing all she had learned about cooking in a Greek kitchen and focusing more on low salt and low sugar meals. It was tough to go against her natural instinct of cooking rich foods, drizzled with olive oil, and fresh feta cheese, but she knew this is what the residents needed. She didn't mind much, though. She was still serving people and making them happy.

I skipped to her car, wearing a She-Ra backpack, purple trimmed glasses, and specially made, Buster Brown shoes to correct my flat footedness. "Hi, *yiayia*!" I said. "*Yiasou*, Matina. Hello! How was your day?" In that short ride to her home, we spoke about our day: what I had learned in school; who I played with at recess; what I had for lunch (which was always met with a frustrated, "*Po, po, po*. Can't they give you kids some real food?"). The ride always ended the same way—with a stop at the local deli. *Yiayia* would give me a crisp, 5-dollar bill and ask me to get cigarettes for her and a treat for myself. I typically opted for Hostess Sno-Balls, drawn to their bright pink color. The deli owner, Mr. Hi, gave me our poison and the change.

We drove up the hill and down *yiayia's* dead-end block. Her home, a humble attached two-family, was snuggled right in the middle of the block. The sterile brown brick exterior and aluminum siding contrasted the warmth found within. From the moment anyone entered *yiayia's* home, they were met with affection. Brown and beige carpet lined the entire home, top to bottom. The formal living room had French provincial furniture, a bright red loveseat, pink club chairs, all dressed in the smoothest velvet fabric and covered in the firmest plastic. Past the living room was the dining room, a small wooden table which often welcomed upwards of thirty people (How did they all fit there?). However, it was into the kitchen and family room that all the magic happened. The linoleum floor and wooden cabinets hugged the hearth of the home, the kitchen. There *yiayia* made all her special treats—her warm butter cookies, her sugar sprinkled almond cookies, her creamy rice pudding, her fluffy carrot cake, and her syrupy desserts. Rosewater and toasted almond always laced the air in *yiayia's* kitchen. Past the kitchen was a tiny family room with a red-brick fireplace. The couches were worn and weathered, showing the years of comfort they provided. Behind the couch was a special drawer where my uncle kept his baseball cards. Across the couches was a small, pleather wrapped bar with four wobbly stools. The bar had classic alcohol selections, *tsipouro*, red wine from Nemea, Chivas Regal, Mavrodaphne liqueur, and so on. Of course, the ouzo took center stage. Two gloriously designed porcelain bottles shaped like a male and female, both dressed in traditional Greek costumes of the *amalia* and *evzona* rested upon a white crocheted runner right beneath the central bar light. Alcohol in Greek households is always placed out in the open, available to any guest that may stop by throughout the day. There was no need to keep it locked up from children; we enjoyed a sip here and there during holidays, anyway.

Yiayia put her bag on the kitchen table and said, "Okay, Matina. I need to take a quick nap. Wake me up at 4 o'clock, right before *Oprah* starts. Make sure you do your homework." I did as I was told, letting my grandma get her much needed rest. Homework came easy to me and thankfully so as there were no adults available to assist me. Mom was busy working at the framing store in Queens, dad was at his car dealership in Brooklyn, and *yiayia* hardly spoke English. I always wondered how she managed to navigate life on Staten Island with a thick accent and limited reading and writing proficiency, but she did. I laid on the carpeted floor, books wrapped in Lisa Frank paper sprawled around me, and an open New Kids on the Block binder before me. I tapped away, completing the ditto worksheet quickly, leaving myself just enough time to read a couple chapters of the latest Babysitters Club book I had recently checked out from the library. When 4 P.M. rolled around, I went upstairs to *yiayia's* bed to wake her, "*Ela, yiayia*. Time to wake up! Oprah is starting in two minutes." "I'm up. I'm up. *Pame kato*. Let's go downstairs to cook."

With every turn of her spoon, *yiayia* offered a lesson. Today's lesson was about being an independent woman. "Leaving the village was not easy. I had a comfortable life. Your grand-*pappou* had made good money as the owner of the *kafenio*, but, sadly, the Nazis destroyed that. They took all we had, but at least they didn't take our lives. So many suffered. I got away with a lot because I was blonde. I learned then that looks, combined with intelligence, can be a powerful combination. My mother and father sent me to America to live with my aunt, who had no children, when I was just 12. Learning a new way of living was not easy. I went to Catholic school and wondered why all the girls were doing their cross the wrong way. But it wasn't about doing a cross, learning math, or writing an essay. It was about opportunity. America gave me the opportunity to be a new person. I wasn't going to be a village wife. I was going to move to a new, exciting land and meet people who had experienced life in different ways."

I listened intently as she described her journey to America, each part of her story bubbling with enthusiasm. I wondered to myself, would I ever become half the woman she was, or was I destined to live a life of mediocrity? And just then, as if she was responding to my thoughts, *yiayia* said, "Matina mou, the world is yours. You have your family's love. You are smart. You are God's child. There is nothing that can stop you from greatness. But, you must always remember, above all, do good in this world. The world needs people who lift others up. Make sure you are that person. Even Socrates, our forefather once said, 'Be kind, for everyone you meet is fighting a hard battle.' Help people win their battles." It was then that I knew that my life's work would involve helping others reach their full potential. The question remained, what form would that take? But, knowing *yiayia*, she had a story for me to figure that out too.

Tim Roda

Tim Roda is an Italian American based in Long Beach, NY. He is an artist and assistant professor at Molloy University. He is known for his multidisciplinary approach to clay and photography that record themes of the family. Roda holds an MFA from the University of Washington, Seattle. He has received several awards, most notably a Fulbright Award to Italy. Roda is the 2012 recipient of the Kennedy Family Fellowship at the University of South Florida, Tampa. He completed residencies at the Archie Bray Foundation, Marie Walsh Sharpe, and the Centro Cultural Andratx. His work is included in the following collections: Bard College Museum, Hessel Foundation; The Rose Museum, Brandeis University; Seattle Art Museum and the Henry Art Museum; Portland Art Museum; Elton John Collection; Museum of Contemporary Photography; Essl Museum; Gaia Collection; and the Centro Cultural Andratx. Reviews of Roda's work have been included in *The New Yorker* magazine, *ARTFORUM*, *Modern Painters* magazine, *Beautiful/Decay*, *Art in America*, and *Slate*.

The home of the author's grandfather, Armondo Antonio Roda, in Rosarni, Italy

EXCERPT

We didn't have cable television because it cost too much, and my parents wanted us to play outside. Our water system was hooked into the solar panels on our roof and to our wood stove. Showers were cold in the summer if the sky was overcast and scalding in the winter if the stove was burning hot. It wasn't unusual for the bread we bought from the discount food store to have mold on the crust. We didn't have presents to open on Christmas morning. Instead, we traveled to Europe, Hawaii, and Mexico. My parents packed canned potatoes, crackers, and individual cups of soup in our suitcase to save money during our trips.

The Immigrant Hustle

[Italian]

Tim Roda

My grandfather, Armondo Antonio Roda, was a first-generation Italian immigrant. He taught me how to hustle. The word hustle has a few meanings, including to hurry someone or something along, a fraud or swindle, or to obtain by forceful action or persuasion. Less commonly known, a hustle is slang for a side job that brings in extra money. When he was 12 years of age, "Papap," as my siblings and cousins affectionately called him, emigrated from Pentidatillo, a remote village in Calabria, Italy. He settled in Lancaster, Pennsylvania where he lived with his family. Growing up, Papap told us stories of how going to school in a new country was difficult. He was picked on for not speaking English. He was beat up and called names because of his accent and Italian background.

Papap's family was poor, yet he had street smarts, a strong work ethic, and a way of making the most of what he had. He passed these traits down to my father and to me.

When I was 10 years old, my grandfather taught me to be resourceful by making money by using what we had on hand. The first hustle I learned was to sell fruit, vegetables, and eggs from our family farm. I set up a table with baskets of apples, pears, figs, nuts, tomatoes, beans, and eggs outside my father's barbershop. Customers had to walk by my stand after getting a haircut. When I was older, Papap taught me to paint houses. He put an advertisement in the local paper and went with me on my first job, first showing me to sand, hold the brush, and use the correct amount of paint. While I worked, he patiently sat nearby. When I tired, he told me to paint with my left hand, a time-saving trick he'd learned over the years. He encouraged me to harvest wild dandelions from the fields surrounding our home and sell at the local farmer's market. They made excellent soup and wine. We also carted our small pony to the nearby retirement home. Residents and their family members could take photos with the pony for a small fee.

Papap influenced my father, too, which led my parents to have their own ideas of how to raise my three siblings and me. Their eccentricities left me, as an adult, often searching for the answer to the age-old questions: What's important in life? and What's the "right way" to live? My father purchased an acre of land from a local farmer in rural Pennsylvania. He and Papap built an A-frame house using scrap materials they found at local second-hand stores. They often frequented dumps near commercial and real estate building sites. My father was well ahead of his time with the farm-to-table concept. Our house was surrounded by corn fields, fruit and nut trees, and a large vegetable garden that fed us year-round. We raised chickens, some of which we kept for egg-laying. The others we ate. We had pet goats and two ponies that ate the grass in our yard, cutting down on mowing time. Our father wanted us to eat steroid-free meat. Every year we raised a calf that we would slaughter when it was of age. The first year, he decided to tackle the massive undertaking himself, using a crosscut handsaw and stacking the severed sections in my sister's bathroom shower stall. The stench of flesh and warm blood lingered in the air for weeks. Twice a year, we held "Chicken Sunday," which was a morning massacre of the plump chickens we'd raised. He sawed off their heads, pulled out the innards, and it was our job to pluck the pinfeathers off carcasses. At the end of the day, my job was to collect the chicken heads so our dog, Max, wouldn't eat them.

We didn't have cable television because it cost too much, and my parents wanted us to play outside. Our water system was hooked into the solar panels on our roof and to our wood stove. Showers were cold in the summer if the sky was overcast and scalding in the winter if the stove was burning hot. It wasn't unusual for the bread we bought from the discount food store to have mold on the crust. We didn't have presents to open on Christmas morning. Instead, we traveled to Europe, Hawaii, and Mexico. My parents packed canned potatoes, crackers, and individual cups of soup in our suitcase to save money during our trips.

Growing up in an Italian American immigrant family had a profound influence on my future career choice to become an artist and art professor. My childhood taught me to think outside of the box, voice my opinions, and realize that being different is good. Navigating the art world and academia is its own type of hustle. Much of my work stems from memories, both real and borrowed from my Papap's life in Italy that I have fused with present day social commentaries. I translate memories and current observations to create a celebration of life in Italy and the United States; at times being satirical about the family spectacle because my childhood was not the norm.

I recently took my four sons and wife to the two-room farmhouse where my grandfather lived as a boy. His home is in the southern-most tip of Italy. To get there, my family and I needed a 4-wheel drive vehicle that followed dry riverbeds, bouncing us around the seats until our backs ached and our teeth rattled. When we couldn't go any farther in the jeep, we journeyed on foot, hiking up the mountain dotted with olive and fig trees until we reached what remained of the home. Much of structure was still intact even though it had been abandoned for decades due to an earthquake that destroyed much of the town. The small house had dirt floors and a large window that overlooked the land leading down to the Ionian Sea. I could imagine my grandfather's donkey, cow, and other animals living on the bottom floor. In this moment of seeing his childhood home for the first time, I finally connected what was real in front of my eyes with the borrowed hours listening to my grandfather's memories of beauty of his land and the struggle it took to survive there.

My work today looks backward to keep my Italian heritage alive and relevant. Most third-generation Italian Americans have assimilated into the American culture. They do not speak fluent Italian or intentionally seek out the stories, people, and places of their Italian beginnings. I strive to make art that works as a bridging agent between my grandfather's past and the present day, intentionally using black and white aesthetics and earthenware clay and other found objects to honor the ways of life that my Calabrian and Italian American family holds dear. My Papap and my father were driving influences for me to become a first-generation college student, to strive to be the first person in my family to earn a master's degree, to apply and be awarded with a Fulbright Award to Italy to practice my craft, and to have the honor of exhibiting my work at the Museum of Contemporary Photography in Chicago or the Seattle Art Museum.

Emanuel Giouroukakis

Emanuel Giouroukakis is the grandson of immigrants on both sides of his family. He is an 11th grader at Manhasset High School and loves reading and writing. He enjoys playing sports, and, in particular, soccer and hockey. He goes to Greece every summer and stays at his family house on the island of Crete. Emanuel attended Greek language school at his local church from pre-kindergarten to grade 8 and is connected to his Greek heritage. He also belongs to the Hellenic Club of his high school which he helped restart with his sister. Emanuel appreciates his ancestors and emulates their key values.

The author at the Acropolis Museum in Athens, Greece

The author's paternal grandfather, Emanuel Giouroukakis, seen here with Senator Teddy Kennedy at a political fundraiser in Astoria, New York

EXCERPT

I am thankful to my grandfather for instilling in me, through example, key character traits that define my identity, and I hope I can do the same thing for my children one day. I wish I could have met my grandfather, but I feel like he is with me in spirit every day of my life.

My Grandfather, the Legend

[Greek]

Emanuel Giouroukakis

Although I was never fortunate enough to have the opportunity to meet my grandfather, Emanuel Giouroukakis, I have always been regaled with legendary tales of his bravery and perseverance in the face of adversity.

My grandfather was known for his tireless work ethic, steadfast determination, and indomitable spirit. Born in 1936, he and his family were forced to relocate from their home in Crete as a result of the German occupation of Greece. They were forced to relocate to a less desirable home in the same village, which caused significant trauma for his family. In the 1950s, he immigrated to the United States in search of a better life. Due to extreme poverty and limited economic opportunities in postwar Greece, he was compelled to leave his family and work on shipping vessels and traveled the world in search of a better life. As one of ten children with one family farm, he needed to leave Greece so he would not be a burden on his family. One such vessel docked in New York City, where he became aware of the presence of a relatively large Greek community in which he saw promise for a better future. He did not speak English or any language other than Greek, so he felt that the United States, the land of opportunity that had embraced other Greek immigrants, would also give him a chance to succeed.

In America, my grandfather settled in Astoria, New York where he subsequently held various jobs as a painter and a furrier. He worked extremely hard to make a living and send money back home to his relatives. In 1968, he met my grandmother, Anna, and they married that same year. In the early 1970s, he established a donut shop, where he worked long hours every single day, except for Christmas and Easter. The donut shop was a local hangout which was frequently visited by loyal members of the Greek community.

My father, who lived in proximity to the shop, has fond memories of spending time there and learning valuable lessons about life. He would take his bike and ride it to the shop every day after school and played in and around the store where he met interesting customers over the years. These customers which included people with varied socioeconomic backgrounds who worked in different jobs and professions (e.g., construction, plumbing, medicine, and law enforcement) and some shady characters, gave him a deep insight into that diverse community. My father would say that he learned a lot of life lessons, sometimes more than what he learned in school.

My grandfather exhibited bravery during his lifetime. During the 1970s and 1980s, the crime rates in New York City were considerably higher than they are today. The donut shop my grandfather owned was located in an area with a high concentration of bars and nightclubs, which often attracted unruly and inebriated individuals. As a result, my grandfather was compelled to take measures to ensure his own safety, such as carrying a handgun when traveling to and from the shop, despite living only a block and a half away. The reason he carried a handgun was because he always carried cash on him from the store, which is a target for robbers. Once, my grandfather encountered two armed robbers who entered the donut shop, so he placed a handgun in his waistband. He was informed by someone that two individuals were there to rob the store, so he came out of the kitchen and showed them the handgun in his waistband. The robbers got frightened and decided to pay for their meal and not rob the store. Another time, my grandfather encountered a drunk person who attacked him without provocation. However, my grandfather defended himself and chased him away.

Through various accounts shared by my father, I have gained an understanding of the challenges my grandfather faced in running the shop, as well as the strategies he employed to deal with these difficulties. Despite his relatively small and unassuming physical appearance, my grandfather possessed a formidable strength and determination, which served him well in defending himself and the shop from potential threats. Despite the challenges posed by operating a business in a working-class area, my grandfather was able to defend himself when necessary. I am grateful for the relative safety and security of my suburban community, which does not entail the same level of challenging traumatic experiences as those faced by my grandfather during his time running the donut shop as an immigrant.

Through his father's example, my father learned the importance of hard work and determination, ultimately becoming a successful lawyer. He named me after his father in accordance with Greek tradition, as my grandfather had passed away prior to my birth. Unlike my father, my grandfather did not receive a formal education, but he had a keen understanding of society and politics and possessed great intelligence and street-smarts.

Unlike my grandfather, I have the ability to go to school and receive an education. I am grateful for this, and I don't take it for granted. In my life, I strive to emulate my grandfather's perseverance and dedication by utilizing these skills in my own life. I am dedicated to my academics, sports, and community. In school, I study hard and for long hours to achieve my goal of exceling in my courses. In both soccer and hockey, I practice for long periods of time to develop my skills and contribute to my team. During games, I give the team my best effort and try to motivate my teammates to achieve our common goal of winning. In terms of my community, it is imperative for me to support it by giving back to those less fortunate. I contribute to my church and help with activities, such as volunteering at the Thanksgiving Food Drive and the Greek Festival.

I am thankful to my grandfather for instilling in me, through example, key character traits that define my identity, and I hope I can do the same thing for my children one day. I wish I could have met my grandfather, but I feel like he is with me in spirit every day of my life.

Paul Giouroukakis

Paul Giouroukakis is the grandson of immigrants on both sides of his family. He attends seventh grade at Manhasset Middle School and loves reading and writing. He enjoys playing sports, and, in particular, soccer and lacrosse. He goes to Greece every summer and stays at his family house on the island of Crete. Paul has been attending Greek school at his local church since PreK and is connected to his Greek heritage. Paul appreciates his grandparents and the love and affection they show him every day.

The author playing backgammon with his grandfather, Polychronis Menexas

EXCERPT

My immigrant grandfather has been living on this earth for 80 years and has shown me everything I know; whether it's cheating in backgammon or showing me what hard work is like. He has brought my family and me closer together, and I wouldn't trade him for the world.

Growing up with a Pappou

[Greek]

by Paul Giouroukakis (age 12)

Growing up with a Greek grandpa, or as Greek people will say, "pappou," gave me an experience that made growing up (and still growing up) extremely lovely and gratifying. My pappou, whom I was named after, immigrated to the United States from Greece in 1969. He overcame all obstacles and is now here with us at age 80, still very healthy.

My pappou is unique. He should be retired, but he works and owns a gyro/pizza place at his age in the Bronx. He has been working since the age of five when he sold newspapers on the train that left the station in his village every morning. He's also cheap to others but generous to me, giving me 100-dollar bills on my birthday. My pappou was poor growing up, so he wants to make sure that we are taken care of and wants us to realize that we are lucky. He is always there for my family and me when we need him.

I remember when my pappou first taught me how to play backgammon the Greek way. He is a cheater sometimes, but I would let him cheat. It made him feel good, and it made me a better player. I remember the day I finally beat him at his own game. I was proud of myself, and he was delighted that I finally knew the ins and outs of the game.

My pappou is very knowledgeable when it comes to soccer and loves the sport. He comes to all my games as well as my siblings' games. He lives in Astoria, NY, a 45-minute drive from Manhasset! Even if the game is at seven in the morning or at night, he is always there to take me and cheer me on. He is my cheerleader. When the referee makes a bad call, he tries to argue with him as much as he can in his Greek-American accent (American with a thick, European accent).

We all talk Greek in the house with each other, and although it is hard for me to understand and respond, I still manage to converse. My family and pappou go to Greece every summer, so it is important to be able to communicate with our relatives. Just like I am learning my pappou's native language, he is working on his English (It isn't perfect, but it does the job.). He's still learning how to speak it, but it is improving as he interacts with people who speak it daily.

My grandma, his wife, died last summer, and it was not only hard for me, but hard for him especially. He lost someone he cared about for 60+ years, and we all care about him as much as he cared about his wife.

My immigrant grandfather has been living on this earth for 80 years and has shown me everything I know; whether it's cheating in backgammon or showing me what hard work is like. He has brought my family and me closer together, and I wouldn't trade him for the world.

CPSIA information can be obtained
at www.ICGtesting.com
Printed in the USA
BVHW022232130623
665930BV00014B/222

9 798765 763834